CAMFRANGLAIS:
The Making of a New Language in Cameroonian Literature

Peter Wuteh Vakunta

Langaa Research & Publishing CIG
Mankon, Bamenda

Publisher:
Langaa RPCIG
Langaa Research & Publishing Common Initiative Group
P.O. Box 902 Mankon
Bamenda
North West Region
Cameroon
Langaagrp@gmail.com
www.langaa-rpcig.net

Distributed in and outside N. America by African Books Collective
orders@africanbookscollective.com
www.africanbookcollective.com

ISBN: 9956-792-96-9

© Peter Wuteh Vakunta 2014

DISCLAIMER
All views expressed in this publication are those of the author and do not necessarily reflect the views of Langaa RPCIG.

Dedication

To victims of linguicide in the Republic of Ongola

Table of Contents

Acknowledgement..vii

Preface.. ix

Chapter 1: The Post-colony writes back..................... 1

Chapter 2: Camfranglais: The Making of a New Language in Cameroon... 59

Chapter 3: The Signifying Monkey: Le Camfranglais, quelle parlure?.. 71

Chapter 4: Literary Camfranglais in Mercédès Fouda's *Je parle camerounais: pour un renouveau francofaune*..................... 81

Chapter 5: Fictionalizing Camfranglais in Fonkou's *Moi taximan*.. 97

Chapter 6: Streetwise French in Nganang's *Temps de chien*..111

Chapter 7: Camfranglais and the Question of Orality in Cameroonian Literature..133

Chapter 8: Conclusion.. 157

Works cited.. 165

Glossary/Glossaire.. 183

Index...215

Acknowledgement

A work of this calibre is, undoubtedly, the end-product of sustained perusal and critiquing of works by peers in the field. This book was inspired by interest in the seminal works of language scholars and linguists in Cameroon, namely André-Marie Ntsobé (2008); E. Biloa (1999); E. Chia (1983, 1992); Jean-Paul Kouega (2013, 2008, 2007); Paul Mbangwana (983, 1987); Simo Bobda, (1994,1999) and Ze Amvela (1989). I owe these genuine intellectuals a debt of gratitude. Portions of several chapters of this book appeared in the following journals: *Translation Review73* (2007), *Meta54.4* (2008), *Midwest Modern Language Association Journal 44.2*(2011), *Journal of African Literature Association* 6.2(2012) and *Pambazuka 574*(2012). For permission to republish, I thank the editors and journals.

Preface

Camfranglais: The Making of a New Language in Cameroonian Literature addresses the emergence of a hybrid code in Cameroon and its usage as a narrative canon in francophone literature. In order to transpose the speech patterns and idiolects of Cameroonians into fictional writing, creative writers consciously deconstruct the French language in an attempt to reflect socio-cultural realities. Linguistic manipulation engenders a third code that poses enormous problems for readers and translators not acquainted with Cameroonianisms. When creative writers resort to linguistic miscegenation as a narrative device they do so in a bid to superimpose the speech particularisms and value systems of indigenes upon a foreign tongue—in our case French. By resorting to the domestication of French the writers whose works constitute the corpus analysed in this book give leverage not just to indigenous languages but also to the kind of streetwise French spoken by the Cameroonian rank and file.

The first chapter of this book theorizes postcoloniality; it delves into theories of post-colonialism and their ramifications for fictional writing after colonization. Chapter Two is a review of Kouega's extensive research on the emergence of a new code in Cameroon—*Camfranglais*. It dwells on the sociolinguistic and morphological structures of this emerging language. Chapter Three explores the trope of *signifying* (or linguistic tricksterism) as a literary canon in Cameroonian literature. It provides readers with an inventory of words and expressions that have come to be accepted as the functional vocabulary of Camfranglophones. Chapter

Four sheds ample light on the phenomenon of linguistic indigenization as a narrative trope in *Je parle camerounais: pour un renouveau francofaune* by Mercédès Fouda. The crux of the discourse in Chapter Five is the fictionalization of Camfranglais in Fonkou's *Moi taximan*. Engaged as he is in the game of language, this Cameroonian writer creates his own language of fiction in a multilingual context affected by signs of diglossia. The kernel of the discourse in Chapter Six revolves around the rationale for recourse to streetwise French in *Temps de chien* by Patrice Nganang. This novel addresses the language question in Cameroonian literature. It focuses on the manner in which the novelist employs code-switching as a narrative strategy in a bid to marry form with content. Chapter Seven discusses the question of orality in Cameroonian literature. It creates a nexus between oral traditions and the print culture in Cameroonian literature. In the conclusion of this work, we contend that fictional writing in a multilingual context such as Cameroon harbors wide-ranging ramifications for creative writers who tend to bestride linguistic divides in an attempt to infuse fictional works with the particularities of indigenous cultures.

The significance of this study resides in its raising awareness to the emergence of a new genre in world literature—hybridized literature. This work rejects the assumption according to which literatures written in less commonly taught languages should be subsumed into one universally accessible global idiom. Instead, *Camfranglais: The Making of a New Language in Cameroonian Literature* asks readers to regard untranslatability as the key to cross-cultural engagement. The book's multiple approaches and innumerable sources generate fascinating connections and provide an excellent introduction to a complex literary phenomenon alien to literati resident outside the Republic of Cameroon.

Chapter 1

The Post-colony Writes Back

For many literary critics, the term "postcolonialism" seems to harbor a double signification. It carries positive overtones when used in reference to the blossoming literatures produced in post-colonies. Conversely, the term tends to be assigned negative connotations when employed as a trope for the dilemmas characteristic of societies that have experienced imperialism: the problems associated with constructing identities in the wake of colonization, and the ways in which writers from previously colonized nations grapple with issues revolving round the articulation of national identities. More often than not, the term is used as a paradigmatic approach for describing the ways in which knowledge, values and cultures of the colonized have been exploited to serve the interests of the ex-colonizer. At the same time, recourse to the term 'post-colonialism' sheds light on the various modes in which the literatures of imperial powers have been used to justify colonialism. Fictional writing serves as a discursive medium through which writers are able to mediate their location inside and outside the colonial culture. Given the ambivalence of this term, a theory of literary postcolonialism should be informed not only by the chronological construction of post-independence, but more by discourse on the experience of imperialism. In this perspective, theorizing literary post-coloniality would be more illuminating if approached from a standpoint that takes into account both the historical and literary perspectives of post-colonialism. As Jacqueline Bardolph points out:

Le premier sens de "postcolonial" est un sens historique, donnant un repère pour les années qui à partir de l'indépendance ... marquent une rupture radicale dans les rapports entre les gouvernements européens et le reste du globe .... Le second sens du terme "postcolonial" définit l'ensemble d'une production littéraire ou même culturelle en ce qu'elle a en commun une langue donnée héritée de la colonisation et à cause de ce passé un certain nombre de traits partagés (10)
[The primary import of the term "postcolonial" is historical, providing a reference point for the period which became a watershed in the relations between European governments and the rest of the world after independence ....The secondary signification of the term defines the totality of literary or even cultural works which have in common a language inherited from colonialism and thus share a number of common traits on account of this historical past][1]

Bardolph's postulations underscore not only the diachronic but also the synchronic aspects of postcoloniality, especially their implications for postcolonial literary theory.

Literary Post-colonialism

The colonial factor continues to be the backdrop against which postcolonial literary productivity occurs. The merger between the oral traditions of indigenous societies and the print culture has engendered hybrid literatures characterized by ambivalence and incessant negotiation of linguistic and cultural spaces. In *The Empire Writes Back* (1989), Ashcroft,

---

[1] All translations are mine except otherwise indicated.

Griffiths and Tiffin define literary post-colonialism in the following terms:

> We use the term 'postcolonial'...to cover all the culture affected by the imperial process from the moment of colonization to the present day. This is because there is a continuity of preoccupations throughout the historical process initiated by European imperial aggression. We also suggest that it is most appropriate as the term for the new cross-cultural criticism which has emerged in recent years and for the disclosure through which this is constituted...What each of these literatures has in common beyond their special and distinctive regional characteristics is that they emerge in their present form out of the experience of colonization and the tension with the imperial power, and by emphasizing their differences from the assumptions of the imperial center. It is this which makes them distinctively postcolonial (2)

The crux of the excerpt above is the fact that writers in post-colonies tend to respond to colonial legacy by writing back to the imperial center from the empire in a bid to express alterity. Thus, the struggle for self-definition and self-determination constitutes the inevitable trajectory toward collective liberation. This comes about as the ex-colonized begin to write their own histories and literatures using the ex-colonizer's language (English, French, Portuguese, and other European languages) for their own purposes. Postcolonial literatures call into question some of the assumptions associated with the colonial era, notably notions of language, culture and nationhood. As Ashcroft, Griffiths, and Tiffin contend, "The idea of postcolonial literary theory emerges from the inability of European theory to deal adequately with the complexities and varied cultural provenance of postcolonial writing" (11). This theoretical deficiency marks the beginning of what Nigerian writer, Wole Soyinka, has characterized as the "process of self-apprehension" (1976: xi). It is this sense of self-interrogation that constitutes each national literature's mode of expression and its aspiration to be self-sustaining. Postcolonial writers tend to take stock of colonialism's impact on the post-colony. They strive to produce works that negate colonialism's philosophical and cultural foci. For example, issues bordering on the impact of assimilationist policies on the psyche of the colonized are recurring themes in novels such as *Le vieux nègre et la médaille* (1956), *Mission terminée* (1957), *Le pauvre Christ de Bomba* (1956) *Climbié* (1956), *Aventure Ambiguë* (1961), *Crépuscule des temps anciens* (1962) and *Things Fall Apart* (1958) among others.

The ideology of sovereignty is articulated in each of the aforementioned novels as a decolonizing paradigm. This choice enables writers to produce works that point in the direction of a critical appraisal of the impact of colonialism on fictional writing in European languages in the post-colony. The study of postcolonial literatures concerns itself with the question of how these literatures bear the imprint of the material forces of cultures, politics and power, and of how postcolonial writers attempt to replace the imperial language within the cultural world of the colonial periphery. The question of language is central in postcolonial literary theorization. It is the centrality of language choice in postcolonial literatures that has spurred literary critic, Ngugi wa Thiong'o, to pose the following perplexing question:

"By our continuing to write in foreign languages, paying homage to them, are we not on the cultural level continuing that neo-colonial slavish and cringing spirit? What is the difference between a politician who says Africa cannot do without imperialism and the writer who says that Africa cannot do without European languages?"(Quoted in Olaniyan & Quayson, 300).

The postcolonial writer's attempt to appropriate the language of the ex-colonizer has led some critics to draw a parallel between Caliban's language of resistance in Shakespeare's *The Tempest* (1959) and the language of the dissident postcolonial writer. The play is set on a mysterious island surrounded by the ocean. Prospero rules the island with his two servants, Ariel and Caliban. When Prospero shipwrecked on the Island, Caliban and Ariel treated him kindly but Prospero later makes them his unwilling servants.

In Scene Two of the play we encounter Prospero and his servants—the self-effacing Ariel, and Caliban, an abrasive, foul-mouthed servant. We are told that while the language of Ariel is that of a slave who binds himself to his master without question, that of Caliban is one that questions the authority of his master as seen in the except below:

You taught me language;
And my profit on't is I know how to curse.
The red plague rid you
For learning me your language!" (1, ii 363-65)

Caliban's language in this passage comes as a shock to Prospero, the more so because it is unexpected that a servant would defy his master in this manner. Caliban's anger toward his master is indicative of his urge to be freed from Prospero's domination. Shakespeare's play sheds light on the dynamics of power in a colonial set-up. The relationship between Prospero and his servants throughout the play supports a colonialist reading of the text. *The Tempest* written in 1611 saw a new dawn in sea travel. It was written two years after the ill-fated journey of the Sea Adventure to Virginia. It is likely that this early attempt at colonization had an influence on Shakespeare's conception of the themes and characterization in his play. The theme of colonialism can be explored further by examining the dynamics of power between Prospero, the supposed 'colonialist' and his 'colonized,' Ariel and Caliban.

The encounter between Caliban and Prospero raises interesting questions about the function of language and power dynamics in postcolonial fictional writing. The play provides one of the most telling demonstrations of the critical importance of language in the colonial encounter. Caliban's reaction to the diatribes of Prospero's daughter, Miranda, encapsulates the malaise and bitter reaction of many colonized peoples to centuries of linguistic and cultural imperialism. Caliban's language is the product of a mind surely in a state of general discomfort and ill ease. Caliban rejects the master's language because Prospero has given him the tools of communication but has failed to give him the freedom and self-responsibility with which to use the language. His rebellious attitude is a reaction to the feeling that he is being abused and subordinated.

This afore-cited excerpt has been upheld by postcolonial theorists as a symbol of linguistic resistance in literatures of decolonization. By appropriating the colonizer's language, Caliban is able to break out of Prospero's infernal linguistic prism. His longing for autonomy makes him relevant in the study of postcolonial Francophone African literature. Like Caliban, African Francophone writers frequently manipulate the French language in a bid to dismantle the power structures that determine the master-servant relationship. By doing so, ex-colonized writers are able to actualize their own possibility of being. Ashcroft et al. posit that this is the "key to the transformative dynamic of postcolonial writing and cultural production" (91).

It is the same craving for liberation that Aimé Césaire fictionalizes in his play, *Une tempête* (1969) in which Caliban denounces his master in vitriolic terms:

> Tu m'as tellement menti,
> Menti sur le monde, menti sur moi-même
> Que tu as fini par m'imposer
> Une image de moi-même
> Un sous développé, comme tu dis,
> Un sous-capable,
> Voilà comment tu m'as obligé à me voir,
> Et cette image, je la hais! Elle est fausse!
> Et maintenant, je te connais, vieux cancer,
> Et je me connais aussi! (88)
> [And you lied to me so much,
> About the world, about yourself [sic],
> That you ended up by imposing on me
> An image of myself:
> Underdeveloped, in your words, incompetent,
> That's how you made me see myself!
> And I loathe that image...and it's false!
> But now I know you, you old cancer,
> And I also know myself! (*A Tempest*, 70]

A critical analysis of the passage above unveils the relationship between language and colonial power; the connection between language and race; and the constitutive, and therefore, putatively ontological power of a dominant language. Like Caliban, the postcolonial writer feels disempowered by borrowed tongues. By appropriating the language of the ex-colonizer and using it to write back to the imperial center, postcolonial writers succeed in actualizing their own ontological being. As Ashcroft points out, this is the "key to the transformative dynamic of postcolonial writing and cultural production" (91). Caliban's reaction to the master's language demonstrates the limits of colonial power. Put differently, imperial power is not absolute but transmutable. Contemporary postcolonial literature harbors the emergence of a language of resistance with the potential to transform the nature of the relationship between the ex-colonizer and the ex-colonized, and consequently the ex-colonizer's power over literary discourse. Like Caliban, the intent of the postcolonial writer is to take hold of the colonial master's language and reconstitute it not simply into a tool of dissidence but also into an instrument of self-representation. It is not just language that the postcolonial writer has to grapple with; language is only the key to a set of power relations that constitute imperial discourse.

Another approach to the study of post-coloniality in literary theory, derived from the works of Frantz Fanon (1959, 1961, and 1967) and Albert Memmi (1965), locates its principal tenet in the imperial/colonial dialectics. In the models propounded by these scholars, the act of writing is subject to the political and social control mechanisms involved in the relationship between the colonizer and the colonized, a relationship that raises important questions, not least of which is the possibility of decolonizing the language of postcolonial literatures. Memmi posits: "La littérature colonisée de langue européenne semble condamnée à mourir jeune," [Colonial literature written in European languages seems doomed to die in its infancy], adding that "Les prochaines générations, nées dans la liberté, écriront spontanément dans leur langue retrouvée" (*Portrait du colonisé*, 166). [Future generations, born in freedom, shall be able to write spontaneously in their lost and found languages.]

Critics of postcolonial literatures have argued that the crucial function of language as a medium for articulating cultural identity in literature demands that postcolonial writing define itself by seizing the language of the center and re-placing it in a discourse fully adapted to the colonized space (Ashcroft et al., 1989; Bhabha, 1990; Rushdie, 1982; Griffiths, 1978; Quayson, 2000; Said 1993; Gandhi, 1998). Identity is constructed through the creation of a third space, in our case, a hybrid language.

Contemporary postcolonial writers attempt to attain this objective by appropriating the language of the ex- colonizer. In practical terms, this is tantamount to recapturing and remolding the colonial language to new usages which mark a separation from the site of colonial privilege. A critical analysis of selected novels in this book lends credibility to contention that the characteristic of "embargoed" literatures is an inevitable tendency towards subversion. The concept of literary "embargo" is used in this book to characterize works of literature written in hybridized and indigenized languages. Although the term "subversion" seems too strong a term to use as a description of the linguistic innovation and experimentation that take place in the works of Cameroonian writers, the fact of the matter is that these writers no longer feel bound by the canons of linguistic conformity associated with the language of the ex-colonizer. As Gérard points out,

> "Their works illustrate a new, forward-looking form of cultural nationalism as they confer dignity and stability to a lingua-franca that derives from a spontaneous oral growth in the autochthonous community" (24).

The following except taken from Fouda's novel illustrates the ex-colonized writer's deliberate attempt to deconstruct metropolitan French by resorting to the use of a home-grown lingua-franca:

> "Chez le soyaman du coin, vous avez passé commande après qu'il vous ait goûté; au moment où il vous faisait le changement, un tonton louche est entré dans votre surface de réparation; vous avez crié à l'agresseur, mais c'était un ninja habillé en western, qui vous a flanqué une raclée mémorable parce que vous avez trop de bouche"(76) [At the soyaman's business premises around the corner, you've placed your order after tasting some of his soya; just when he is about to give your change, a suspicious man invades your comfort zone; you cry for help, only to realize that he is a ninja dressed in Western garb. He gives you a good thrashing because you're too mouthy.]

This excerpt may appear opaque to non-speakers of camfranglais[2] on account of the language mixing. The pidgin

---

[2]Kouega defines Camfranglais as '... a composite language variant, a type of pidgin that blends in the same speech act linguistic elements drawn first from French and secondly from English, Pidgin English and

word "soyaman" derives from two words "soya" and "man" "Soya" is a type of meat roasted on a grill over a fire in the streets, often near bars and night clubs in Cameroon. The term "tonton" is the Cameroonian version of the French word "oncle" but in Fouda's novel, it is used in reference to any unknown fellow. The word "changement" describes the change one receives after giving a salesman a banknote. To fully comprehend the passage above, the reader has to be familiar with the lexicon of this nascent Cameroonian language. The mixing of words such as "soyaman," "western," "tonton," and "ninja" may complicate matters for a monolingual reader of the text. Over and above, the semantic shift evident in the use of words like "goûté," and "changement" is likely to pose comprehension problems as well. In the Cameroonian context, the verb "goûter" is often used to translate the notion of having a taste of food, meat, etc. before buying it. In *Je parle camerounais*, Fouda provides readers with the opportunity to read the kind of Africanized French that is spoken in the streets and neighbourhoods in Cameroonian major cities.

This new trend in literary creativity illustrates what has been described by critics of postcolonial literatures as an irresistible drive toward creative writing that parts with its original elite character, concerns itself with the problems and conditions of the widening circles of readers in the language that they really speak (Griffiths, 1978; Jameson, 1991; White, 1993; Lawson and Tiffin, 1998; Gover et al., 2000). Postcolonial writers endeavour to distance themselves, to a

---

other widespread languages in Cameroon' (2003). He further notes that Camfranglais was purposefully developed by secondary school students in a bid to freely communicate among themselves to the exclusion of non-initiates.

certain degree, from the conventions of imperial literary creativity through the process of literary indigenization as the following except from Fonkou's novel illustrates:

> "Les premiers contacts avec les mange-mille et les gendarmes coûtent cher, mais par la suite, tout le monde se connaît et il s'établit comme un contrat tacite"(12)
> [The first encounter with the mange-mille and gendarmes is costly, but eventually, people get to know one another, and friendship is established tacitly.]

The compound word 'mange-mille' is derived from the two words: 'manger' and 'mille'. It is a derogatory term used by speakers of camfranglais to describe corrupt Cameroonian police officers notorious for taking bribes from taxi drivers, generally in the neighbourhood of 1000 CFA francs, though they would take less when times are hard. "Gendarmes" are the French equivalent of policemen in English-speaking countries. Certain camfranglais neologisms are hard to decipher unless the reader is familiar with the lexicon from which the words are culled. As Ntsobé, Achu, and Biloa caution, "Il faut absolument connaître la signification de ces mots dans leurs contextes spécifiques" (90). [One really has to know the meanings of these words in their specific contexts.] The difficulty stems from the fact that camfranglophones frequently borrow from indigenous languages as this proverbial expression shows: "L'enfant qui vit près de la chefferie ne craint pas le 'mekwum'" (14) [A child who lives near the chief's palace does not fear the 'mekwum'.] The native tongue word 'mekwum' refers to a masked dancer belonging in a secret society in the palace of the village chief.

There are two distinctive processes by which literary indigenization may be achieved. The first is the abrogation or deconstruction of the privilege of the colonial language as seen in the examples above. This involves the rejection of metropolitan control over means of communication. The second is the appropriation and reconstruction of the imperial language to respond to local communication needs as seen in this example from Fouda's novel: "J'ai seulement un 'papa-j'ai grandi' et les 'sans confiance'" (37)[I only have a 'papa-I-have-grown up' and a pair of 'no-confidence.'] A 'papa-j'ai grandi' is a pair of trousers that appear too short or too small on the wearer because s/he has grown bigger. Cameroonians often employ this expression as a form of mockery and, especially as a reminder to the person wearing the pants that it is time to discard them and buy a new pair. 'Sans confiance' is a term employed by Cameroonians to describe low quality rubber-made slippers whose strings can snap without warning. The term 'sans confiance' is often abbreviated as 'sans kong.' 'Sans confiance' literally means 'no confidence.'

As these examples indicate, linguistic appropriation is a necessary step in the process of ensuring that the decolonization of postcolonial literatures comes to fruition. It is a process by which an alien language is taken and made to bear the imprint of one's lived experience and worldview. On the other hand, abrogation is a rejection of the 'sacrosanct' rules of the imperial language, its esthetics, its illusory standards of normative or "correct" usage, and its assumption of a traditional and fixed meaning inscribed in the words of its language. But without appropriation the moment of abrogation may not extend beyond a reversal of the assumptions of privilege.

In the process of literary indigenization, language is adopted and utilized in various ways to express widely differing cultural experiences, for in one sense, all postcolonial literatures are cross-cultural given that they negotiate a space between two different cultural spheres. In his discussion on hybridity, Bhahba (1990) provides a link between resistance and the notion of third space: "The process of cultural hybridity gives rise to something different, something new and unrecognizable, a new area of negotiation of meaning and representation" (211). Postcolonial literatures are often written out of a tension between the abrogation of the European language which speaks from the center, and the act of appropriation which brings it under the influence of an indigenous language. Okara's attempt in *The Voice* to bring the English language under the influence of Yoruba by adapting Ijaw syntax to English is a good example. This exercise enables the creative writer to express his Yoruba imagination through the medium of English. Looking at the various ways in which Okara uses the word "inside" in his novel one is able to make some very clear deductions from the passage about the holistic nature of the "self" in Ijaw language and culture.

In the same light, Patrice Nganang appropriates French by bringing it under the influence of Cameroonian indigenous language modes of speech. He interpolates indigenous language lexes into the French language as seen in the following example: "Menmà, si j'avais encore ta force, j'aurai fait autre chose que de m'asseoir derrière mon comptoir et regarder passer la vie!" (*Temps de chien*, 148) [Menma, if I still had your strength, I'd have done something other than sit behind my counter and watch life go by! (*Dog Days*, 101-2)] The word "Menma" is an Africanism borrowed from the

Medùmba language spoken in Cameroon. It could be translated as "brother or sister," with a dose of affection. By having recourse to a native tongue lexeme, Nganang is able to convey the notion of filial relationship and love to his readers through the prism of his native language. He personifies the word "life" in his text by endowing it with the quality of locomotion in order to emphasize African belief in man's dependence on the cosmos. Nganang's attempt at domesticating the French language is evident in his imitation of local speech patterns as seen in the following passage:

> Regardez-moi un énergumène comme ça qui vient dans un bar comme celui-ci où les gens me respectent dire que c'est lui qui me gère, *anti zamba ouam*! Il ose même dire qu'il voulait m'épouser. Regardez donc le mari de Mini Minor. Dites-moi vraiment, vous qui me connaissez: est-ce que je mérite un têtard comme ça…? Vraaaiiiiment, même les cauchemars ont des limites. Moi la femme de ce cancrelat-ci! (66)
> [But the rest of you, just look at this raving lunatic, who comes into a bar like this where people respect me and says that he is keeping me, *anti zamba ouam!* He even dares to say he wants to marry me. Take a look at Mini Minor's husband. Now tell me, you all who know me: do I deserve a polliwog like that? …. Reeeeally, even nightmares have limits! Me the wife of this cockroach!]
> (*Dog* Days, 44)

The exclamatory "vraaaiiiiment" in this quotation is calqued on oral discourse in Cameroon. Nganang strives to reproduce the elocutionary mannerisms of his French-speaking compatriots. The invocatory expression "anti zamba ouam" is an act of swearing borrowed from the Beti vernacular language spoken in Cameroon. "Zamba" means God Almighty. The speaker is asking God to come to her assistance in the embarrassing situation in which she finds herself. The expression *"anti zamba ouam"* could be translated as "Oh, my God!" These examples show that postcolonial writers tend to employ a variety of indigenization modalities, including vernacular transcription and code-switching, semantic shifts and neologisms among others in a bid to manipulate the standardized form of the ex-colonizer's language. At the same time, this enables them to construct a culturally meaningful discourse.

Kourouma employs similar devices to achieve palpable results as seen in the following extract from *Les soleils des indépendances*:

> Fama et ses deux femmes occupaient la petite pièce avec un seul lit de bamboo, un seul tara ....Avez-vous déjà couché sur un tara? Il grince, geint comme si vous rouliez sur les feuilles mortes d'un sous-bois en plein harmattan" (158)
> [Fama and his two wives lived in the little room, with its one tara or bamboo bed ... .Have you ever slept on a tara? It creaks and crackles as if you were rolling about in a heap of dry leaves in the middle of the harmattan season] (*The Suns of Independence*, 106)]

This passage provides a cultural context for Kourouma's prose narrative. The Malinke word "tara" which the English language translator renders as "bamboo bed" is culturally significant. Bamboo beds are a symbol of social status in traditional Africa. Regional specificity is conveyed in the text through the narrator's reference to the harmattan season, a dry dusty wind that blows along the northwest coast of Africa.

Indigenization of language employed as a writing canon is noticeable in *Les soleils des indépendances* from the very onset. Right from the opening passage, Kourouma introduces the reader to the Malinke mode of speech: "Il y avait une semaine qu'avait fini dans la capitale Koné Ibrahima, de race malinké, ou disons-le en Malinké; il n'avait pas soutenu un petit rhume..." (7) [One week has passed since Ibrahima Koné, of the Malinke race, has met his end in the capital city, or to put it in Malinke, he'd been defeated by a mere cold...] (*The Suns of Independence*, 3). There are several oral elements in this sentence: the formulaic opening, "il y avait une semaine," the emphatic verb "avait fini," the use of the pronoun, "nous" to bridge the gap between narrator and narratee and finally the proverbial expression, borrowed from the Malinke language, "Il n'avait pas soutenu un petit rhume." Kourouma's linguistic indigenization strategy may appear gratuitous, even fortuitous, to the undiscerning eye yet it is a deliberate attempt by the writer to infuse his Francophone text with Malinke speech particularisms. Arguing along the same lines, Magdeleine Borgomano points out: "l'esthétique de Kourouma n'est pas le fruit inattendu d'une production ex-nihilo, mais l'aboutissement prévisible d'une recherche formelle ..." (159) [Kourouma's esthetic is not the unexpected fruit of an ex-nihilo act of creation but the predictable end product of formal research....]

These examples show that the decolonization process in postcolonial literatures resides in the willful subversion of the grammatical norms of European languages. African writers attempt to dismantle what they perceive as the power structures of the imperial language, structures themselves metonymic of the hegemonic control exercised by the ex-colonizer over the ex-colonized in the neo-colony. These writers tend to adopt various strategies by means of which the European language could be manipulated from within. Whether written in diglossic or polyglossic contexts, postcolonial literatures are often intended to call into question the peripheral position accorded the language and culture of the ex-colonized. The language employed by postcolonial writers signifies otherness; but at the same time it ensures a sameness that allows it to be understood beyond the empire. As Ashcroft and Tiffin observe, these writers do this "by employing language variance, the part of a wider cultural whole, which assists in the work of language seizure whilst being neither transmuted nor overwhelmed by its adopted vehicle" (50).

African writers who write in European languages employ these languages as media through which the reader could be introduced to features of culturally diverse postcolonial societies. However, when readers belong in different cultural spheres as is the case with the readers of postcolonial literatures, two issues come to the forefront: can writing in one language convey the reality of a different culture? And can a reader fully comprehend a cultural reality that has been transposed into a different language? The discursive event and the use of language become issues of paramount importance in postcolonial writing. This is evident when the appropriation of language creates a new discourse. In this regard, postcolonial writers run the risk of constructing a discourse that straddles the divide between regional and standardized forms of the languages they are using as channels of expression. For example, the non-Bwa reader would be hard pressed to unravel the underlying signification of the word "soleil" when Nazi Boni writes: "La vieille! N'avait-elle pas fait son soleil et cassé des dizaines d'amphores?" (67) [Had the old lady not done her sun and broken tens of pots?] The difficulty arises from the fact that the narrator translates Hakani's mother's thoughts directly from the Bwa language into French, playing with the expression "to do one's sun," which means "spend one's youth." There is a semantic shift in the use of "soleil" in this context. The technique of selective lexical fidelity whereby the writer leaves some words untranslated in the text is employed effectively throughout *Crépuscule des temps anciens* to underscore cultural distinctiveness. Such a device not only accentuates the difference between cultures; it also illustrates the importance of culture-specific language usage in literature. Boni's use of untranslated Bwa words in his narrative serves as an indication that the language which informs his text is Bwamu. This forces the reader to engage the text from an ethnographic cultural perspective in order to comprehend the import of indigenous language terms and expressions. This is because a full understanding of the text requires the reader's interpretation of the cultural cues beyond the text. In this light, reading becomes an hermeneutic process of interpreting the textual and non-textual elements that account for the holistic meaning of the text.

Post-colonial literary theory puts a premium not only on the importance of discourse analysis but also on the vital link between meaning and contextual usage within the discursive event. In the excerpt discussed above, cultural differentials are not inherent; rather they are created by means of writing canons. Words like "soleil" and "tara" generate semantic nuances which are only accessible through an understanding of the use of vocabulary in context. Ultimately, the domestication of European languages in postcolonial literary texts may be viewed as a manifestation of cultural nationalism; the more so because native-tongue words give the source language culture a higher status than the adopted culture as seen in the work of Congolese writer, Henri Lopès. He strives to domesticate the French language in his seminal novel titled *Le Pleurer-Rire* (1982). From the very first sentence in the novel he strives to indigenize the French language; in short, he writes not only as a literary translator but also as a culture broker as seen in the following example: "Le damuka s'était réuni dans une venelle de Moundié: avenue Général-Marchand" (14) [The wake was held in a little alley in Moundie: the Avenue General-Marchand] (*The Laughing Cry*, 1). The meaning of the word "damuka" in this passage may be lost to the non-Lingala[3] speaking reader of the text. This first sentence sets the tone for the intralingual translation task that awaits the reader of Lopès' text. Sometimes, the narrator performs this task for the reader. When one of the priests conferring traditional authority on Tonton Bwakamabé Na Sakkadé declares: "Boka litassa dountouné!" (47), the narrator comes to the aid of non-Lingala readers by translating the sentence for them as follows: "Ce qu'on peut traduire en français par: "Reçois le pouvoir des ancêtres" (47) [Which could be translated into English as: "Receive the powers of the ancestors"] (*The Laughing Cry*, 21).

Other Africanized French expressions in the text include: "La bouche, la bouche c'est seulement pour la bouche et la parlation que nous, là, on est fort. C'est ça même, mon frère,

---

[3]Lingala is an indigenous language spoken in the Democratic Republic of the Congo, the Republic of the Congo and in some parts of Angola and the Central African Republic.

ô. Nègre, il connaît bien pour lui bouche-parole." (42) [These blacks, really, they are not serious. Just lip, lip—it's only in lip and palaver that we are strong. Too true, brother-o! Blackmen know not'in but mout', mout'] (*The Laughing Cry*, 21). The expressions "bouche-parole" and "parlation" are indigenized French expressions that could be rendered in standard French as "de pure forme" or "en parole" and translated into English as" lip-service." As these examples suggest, Lopès appropriates the French language by using an abridged syntax which characterizes the spoken word in Lingala. Most of the Africanisms in his novel are culled directly from Lingala, thus endowing the text with local flavor and esthetics. Of extreme importance to Lopès is the appropriation of the French language which is used to express the African imagination and worldview. Irele notes that the term "African imagination" should be taken as "referring to a conjunction of impulses that have been given a unified expression in a body of literary texts" (*The African Imagination*, 4). From these impulses, grounded in both common experience and in common cultural references, African literary texts have come to assume a particular significance.

Lopès' language is intended to illustrate not only the specific fictional universe which it contributes to create but also the cultural context in which creative writing is done. This is the reason he makes his characters speak in their own native languages through the prism of the French language. In the course of the narrative Lopès translates native-tongue words and expressions into French for communicative expediency as seen in the following passage:

Tu parles! Commentait Elengui. Aux heures des émissions en kissikini un professeur de physique de cette tribu déclara: "*Mana foléma, mana toukare lowisso natina,*" qui peut être traduit en français par: "Nous luttons résolument contre le racisme."(224)
[So you say! Observed Elengui. At the time reserved for the kissikini programs, a physics professor of that tribe declared: "*Mana foléma, mana toukare lowisso natina,*" which could be translated as "We shall all fight resolutely against racism.](*The Laughing Cry,* 152)

In an interview Lopès granted Denyse de Saivre, he explains some of the motivations that led him to make the kinds of stylistic choices that the reader notices in his novel:

J'ai voulu trouver le ton qu'emploie le peuple lorsqu'il parle de sa vie quotidienne aujourd'hui en Afrique, et c'est ce ton là que j'ai essayé d'imiter...*Le Pleurer-Rire,* qu'est ça veut dire? C'est presque du petit nègre. C'est le français créolisé avec la saveur que nos peuples savent y mettre. Et c'est la manière de dire du peuple que j'ai essayé d'imiter. Le peuple, lorsqu'il se trouve dans des conditions difficiles dans nos pays, préfère utiliser l'humor.... L'humor...c'est une philosophie que je tire de la culture de nos peuples. Toute tradition orale, les contes jusqu'à "Radio-trottoir"en passant par le chant, en est émaillée. (121-22)
[I wanted to adopt a tone that our people use when they talk about their daily lives in Africa today. And it is that tone that I have tried to imitate. *The Laughing Cry* means what? It's a sort of pidgin French. It's creolized French with the flavor that our people are adept at bringing to a

language. And it's the speech mannerisms of the people that I have tried to simulate. In our country, when people find themselves in awkward situations, they prefer to use humor….Humor…is a philosophy that I have borrowed from the culture of our people. All oral art forms, from folktales to "Radio grapevine" and songs are spiced with humor.]

While postcolonial writing has led to the proliferation of literary techniques which exist to span the purported gap between the writer and the prospective reader, the process of writing itself remains a continual process of contextualization and adjustment directly linked to the constitutive nature of meaning and the transformative use of language. Ashcroft makes a pertinent point when he notes: "While meaning in texts is socially constituted, difference and alterity may be similarly constituted within the transformed discourse" (75). There is sound reasoning in Ashcroft's assertion given that cultural experiences could be vastly different, and this difference, as well as the communication of otherness, is itself a feature of postcolonial writing. Alterity is transposed into literary texts by means of language variance which has a metonymic function[4] in postcolonial literatures. Metonymic functionality stems from the semantic gap— the gap created when appropriators of a colonial language insert unglossed words, phrases or passages from a first language, or concepts, allusions or references which may be unknown to the reader. Such words become synecdochic of the writer's culture—the part that stands for the whole. The inserted word stands for

---

[4]Metonymy is a trope in which concepts are referred to not by their names but rather by the names of something else associated in meaning with them.

the colonized culture, and its very resistance to interpretation constitutes a gap between the writer's culture and the imperial culture.

The local writer is able to represent his or her cultural background to the ex-colonizer (and others) in the metropolitan language, and at the same time, to signal and underscore relational differences. According to Ashcroft, the writer is saying: "I am using your language so that you will understand my world, but you will also know by the differences in the way I use it that you cannot share my experience" (75). The distinctive trait of the cross-cultural texuality is the inscription of alterity as a corollary of cultural identity. Consequently, whenever the strategy of linguistic appropriation is used as a literary canon, that is, the device that enables the writer to domesticate the imperial language and use it in a way that transforms discourse into a cultural vehicle for the writer, there is an installation of difference at the very site of meaning in the text. This occurs, perhaps paradoxically, in the use of translation which attempts to eliminate the cultural gap installed through language usage.

Translation and postcolonial theory

The translational strategies by which indigenous languages and cultures are transposed into European languages are varied. Apart from direct glossing in the text, either by explanation or parenthetical insertions, other devices include syntactic fusion, in which the European language prose is structured according to the syntactic principles of an indigenous language; neologisms, new lexical forms in the European language which are informed by the semantic and morphological exigencies of a native tongue; the direct insertion of un-translated lexical items in the text and the transcription of dialects and language variants. These manipulative strategies play the significant role of reproducing the source-language culture through the process of metonymic embodiment. Writers believe that by resorting to these paradigmatic devices they are keeping faith with their indigenous cultures though writing in an 'alien' language. However, this task is often not a sinecure as the subsequent chapters will show.

Arguing along the same lines in the foreword to his novel, *Kanthapura* (1938), Raja Rao sheds light on the particular odds faced by writers in conveying cultural individualism in indigenous liteartures written in foreign languages:

> The telling has not been easy. One has to convey in a language that is not one's own the spirit that is one's own. One has to convey the various shades and omissions of a certain thought-movement that looks maltreated in an alien language. I use the word 'alien,' yet English in not really an alien language to us. It is the language of our intellectual make-up—like Sanskrit or Persian was before—but not of our emotional make-up. We are all instinctively bilingual, many of us writing in our own language and English. We cannot write like the English. We should not. We cannot write only as Indians (Foreword, vii).

Like Rao, most Cameroonian writers are bilinguals for whom French and English are languages of their intellectual rather than emotional make-up. Because of this linguistic dualism they cannot write like the French or the English. Indeed, they should not because creative writing is an embodiment of cultural syncretism. For this reason, they attempt to generate an inter-language through the fusion of the linguistic structures of two languages as seen in this excerpt from *Moi taximan*: "Je ne mangeais chez moi que le soir, sauf les jours où je me faisais aider par un 'attaquant'…afin de me reposer un peu" (18) [I ate at home only in the evening, except on days when I asked an 'attacker' to replace me… so that I could get a little rest.] The narrator employs the word 'attaquant' to describe a taximan who not only works overtime but is often aggressive and easily gets into road rage. Readers of *Moi taximan* who are not familiar with camfranglais may lose the narrative thread when French words are attributed different significations as this other example shows: "On sortait de l'opération avec un plus grand sourire si, en plus, les passagers longue distance avaient 'proposé'…." (8) [At the end of this operation we wore broad smiles if in addition to paying the normal fare, long distance commuters had proposed.] A little further, Fonkou sheds light on the meaning of the word 'proposé': "… payer plus cher que le tarif normal" (8) [Pay more than the normal fare.] This linguistic innovation is not unique to Cameroonian fiction writers.

In his first novel *The Palm-Wine Drinkard* (1952), Nigerian writer Amos Tutuola achieved a similar feat as seen in the following passage:

> I was a palm-wine drunkard since I was a boy of ten years of age. I had no other work more than to drink palm-wine in my life. In these days we did not know other money except COWRIES, so that everything was very cheap, and my father was the richest man in town (7)

Tutuola's style may come as a linguistic shock to purists but to the average Nigerian reader, this novel is a true reflection of daily parlance. Some linguists have described this sort of pidginized English as "inter-language," a coinage by Nemser (1971) and Selinker (1972) to characterize the discrete linguistic system employed by learners of a second-language. This third code along with its concomitant features of inscription, characterizes Tutuola's process of appropriation of the English language through the technique of indigenization. The English in *The Palm-Wine Drinkard* is the literal translation of the writer's native Yoruba tongue into the English language. What Tutuola accomplishes is an approximate form which is distinct from both Standardized English and Yoruba. It is an evocative and culturally rich code. Tutuola turns his unsophisticated English into a weapon of linguistic empowerment on account of his constant borrowing from Yoruba oral traditions and cosmology. The narrator's simplicity of language recreates the speech of a folktale narrator. As such, his text may not be the linguistic aberration it has sometimes been taken to be, but an important example of creative innovation in postcolonial literatures.

The most effective method of achieving creative novelty in postcolonial writing is by employing the technique of code-switching. Switching between two or more codes is a way of installing cultural relativism into works of fiction as illustrated in the writing of Australian novelist Joseph Furphy. This writer demonstrates a brilliant use of the strategy of code-switching in his novel titled *Such is Life* (1903). In this text, the aggregation of so many variants operates to give the sense of a language in the process of mutation. Furphys's characters include the patrician bullock-driver Willoughby, who is here discussing some national heroes with another bullocky, Mosey:

> "Now, Mosey," said Willoughby, courteously but tenaciously.
> "Will you permit me to enumerate a few gentlemen—gentlemen, remember—who have exhibited in a marked degree the qualities of the pioneer. Let us begin with those men of whom you Victorians are so justly proud—Burke and Wills. Then you have—"
> "Hold on, hold on," interrupted Mosey. Yer knocking yerself bad, an' you know it. Wills was pore harmless week, so he kin pass; but look 'ere—there ain't a drover, nor yet a bullock driver, nor yet a stock-keeper from 'ere to 'ell that couldn't,'a' bossed that expegition straight through the Guff, an' back agen an' never turned a hair—with sich a season as Burke had." (32-33)

There is a socio-cultural contest being translated into this dialogue for which language variance is synecdochic. The very concept of national heroes is embedded in a particular kind of discourse of power for which Willoughby's language is itself a signifier. On the other hand, Mosey's pidginized English is symbolic of the social class to which he belongs and the culture that goes with it. Furphy's novel is laden with such language mixings, variants which directly propose cultural hybridity. Variance in his novel is a signifier of otherness. At the same time, it indicates a very complex dynamic of appropriation in these cultures. The continued opposition of the two discourses underlies the psychological characteristics of the societies in question, especially their obsession with nationalism.

Code-switching is perhaps one of the most effective strategies of linguistic appropriation at the disposal of postcolonial writers. It enables them to make the interlanguage bear the burden of an experience for which the terms and experiences of the inherited language do not seem appropriate. Fonkou makes abundant use of code-switching in *Moi taximan* as this statement shows: "Non, un bon bita kola et un matango coupé d'odontol." (120) [No, a nice bitter kola and some matango mixed with odontol.] This sentence is a hybrid code comprising French, Pidgin English and native tongue words. The word "bita kola" is pidgin derived from bitter kola, a species of kola nut noted for its aphrodisiacal qualities. "Matango" is another pidginized word that describes palm-wine. "Odontol," an indigenous language word, refers to locally brewed whiskey. Code-switching occurs when the Empires writes back, as Aschcroft, Griffiths, and Tiffin would have it, by directly transcribing pidginized and creolized forms of imperial languages into postcolonial texts. Dennis Walder defines the term 'pidgin' as a "simplified mixture of two or more languages current in trading or contact situations, but without necessarily being anyone's first tongue" (46). The pidgin used in Achebe's novels, particularly *No Longer at Ease* (1960), *Arrow of God* (1964), and *A Man of the People* (1967), is noteworthy. Other examples are the forms developed on the plantations in the Caribbean for communication between white overseers and their black, mainly West African slaves, involving English, French and Spanish, as well as Ibo, Yoruba, Fanti and other local tongues.

Another example, the Tok Pisin (Pidgin Talk) of Papua New Guinea has expanded and stabilized to an extent that has made it viable as an established lingua-franca with an official status. So too has Gullah[5,] pidgin spoken by a distinct group of African Americans in the southeastern United States, notably the Sea Islands of South Carolina and northern Georgia. A pidigin is a language that is spoken among peoples none of whom are native speakers of it. Walder points out that it is important to distinguish between pidgins, which have small vocabularies, restricted structures, lack expressive potential and are usually not a first language, and creoles which are distinctive varieties of English or French spoken as a vernacular tongue by native speakers. A pidgin becomes creole when people have entirely abandoned their ancestral languages and wholly adopted the pidgin, so that it is the first language of their children. There is some pidgin discourse in Achebe's *Arrow of God* (1964). Winterbottom asks his servant what the singing children are saying as the wind and thunder rise. "Dem say make rain come quick quick" (30-31). In this quotation, the pronoun "dem" replaces "they," "them," "their," and "theirs." "Make" is an imperative or wish: "make rain come" could be rendered as "let rain come!" This is the most common use of "make" in West African Pidgin English. Finally, "quick quick" is one of two kinds of reduplication[6]. In this case, the repetition is an intensifier: "very quick, immediately." Other reduplications exist in Achebe's text. For example, the modest comment of Clarke's cook: "I de try small small "

---

[5]For more on this, read Vakunta's article, "American Gullah, Cousin to West African Pidgin English?"culled April 18, 2014 from http://www.postnewsline.com/2010/06/american-gullah-cousin-to-west-african-pidgin-english.html

[6]Reduplication consists in repeating the root or stem of a word. Oftentimes, it is the entire word that is repeated in order to indicate intensification or plurality. Reduplication conveys such grammatical changes.

(105). The intensifier "small small" could be translated as "little by little" or "piecemeal". Cameroonians use the intensifier "small small" in daily discourse as this wise saying suggests : "Small small, catch monkey," which could be translated as : bit by bit an objective is attained. "De" functions as an indicator of progressive action in the quote taken from Achebe's *Arrow of God*. It means : "I am in the process of..."

Nganang follows in Achebe's footsteps by inscribing Cameroonian Pidgin words and expressions into his French language text. The innovative use of French in *Temps de chien* serves as an indicator that the socio-cultural dichotomies created by colonialism in Cameroon did not disappear with the advent of independence. Pidgin brings flavor to non-standard speech. For example, Nganang's narrator, Mboudjak, makes a remark about one of the characters, Crow, using pidgin diction as seen in the following excerpt: "...maintes fois j'avais vu Docta avec des femmes six fois plus volumineuses que lui. A côte d'elles, il n'était qu'un longo longo fil de fer" (74). [... many times I've seen Docta with women six times his size. Next to them, he was nothing but bones, just a longo longo fil de fer.] (*Dog days*, 50) The word "Docta" is pidgin derived from the English word "doctor." It is generally used in reference to a physician or intellectual holding a doctorate degree. In Nganang's novel, the narrator uses this term as an honorific title for the philosopher, *l'homme en noir noir*. Another pidgin word used in this excerpt is "longo longo" derived from the English word "long." The narrator resorts to the technique of reduplication in a bid to create a qualifier that describes someone who is tall and lanky. The linguistic hybridity in this passage bears testimony to the fact that Nganang's characters are proficient in both English and French. Recourse to code-switching is the writer's attempt at decolonizing the contemporary Cameroonian novel; this technique underscores the need to be oneself and project one's true socio-cultural values through the medium of literature. Nganang mixes multiple languages, the same way Achebe does by copiously injecting both Ibo cultural artefacts and words into his English language novels. Both Nganang and Achebe are influenced by their bicultural upbringings.

The use of code-switching as a narrative trophe in *Temps de chien* goes beyond just being creative with language to sending a message to readers about how Cameroonian society has become hybridized. Nganang adopts a very original narrative technique to illustrate the inner turmoil that Africans experience from cultural imperialism after independence. He deconstructs the French language in order to make this language carry the weight of his Cameroonian experience. What one reads in *Temps de chien* is a reflection of how ordinary Cameroonians communicate on a daily basis. By writing this novel the way he did, Nganang exposes the monolingual reader to other forms of writing and to the different ways in which European languages are spoken on a daily basis in Africa.

Temps de chien is a fascinating text because it brings the African way of life from the cities of Cameroon into a literary focus. The novelist's style reminds the monolingual reader that they are reading a novel conceived in a hybrid culture with many languages, codes, and dialects. The novel would be culturally arid if it did not include all of the complex words and expressions giving the reader an accurate picture of Cameroon's multiculturalism. What we see Nganang's stylistics accomplishing is obligating the monolingual reader to think outside his purview and reading beyond the text in order to comprehend the deeper significations embedded in the author's word choices. Using more than one language in one single sentence seems to be a way of life in Cameroon.

Another Cameroonian writer, Nyamnjoh, avails himself of the technique of code-switching as a narrative device in his book of short stories, *Stories from Abakwa* (2007). These stories are a remarkable depiction of the socio-cultural realities of Mimboland[7], a fictional country that could easily represent his native land, Cameroon. Nyamnjoh does more than re-write the events that characterize the day-to-day preoccupations of people in Mimboland in the post-independence era. The thing that strikes the reader the most in his prose narrative is the language manipulation that takes place in the text. Camfranglais—the hybrid language that not only baffles the protagonist, Fineboy Ayuk, but also leads to his unanticipated demise, is the hallmark of the code-switching that Nyamnjoh wields as a narrative technique:

> "Montre-moi vos pièces!" The taller of the officers startled the inattentive old man when he came up to where they stood. Fineboy Ayuk failed to understand him, and confessed.
> "I no di hear Kampha talk sah."
> "Who di parlez Kampha talk avec toi? I no want nonsense you hear?" The very officer replied full of bile and pulling his ear demonstratively.
> "Sorry sah if I don tonton talk bad talk. But I no di hear dat talk you talk so," Fineboy pleaded with humility.

---

[7]This term was coined by Francis Nyamnjoh in his novel *Married but Available*(2009) to depict his native land, Cameroon, a country where people seek solace in alcoholism.

"Arrêtez-lui...Arrête le fainéante. Search-am fine fine," the officer shouted to his counterpart. (86-87)
["Show me your particulars!' The taller of the two officers said, startling the inattentive old man when he came up to where they stood. Fineboy Ayuk did not understand him and confessed.
"I don't understand Kampha language, sir."
"Who is speaking Kampha language to you? I don't want to hear nonsense from you, do you understand me?" the very officer replied full of bile and pulling his ear demonstratively.
"I am sorry sir, if I have inadvertently said something offensive. But I don't understand the language you are speaking," Fineboy pleaded with humility.
"Arrest him...Arrest the idler. Search him thoroughly," the officer shouted to his counterpart.]

As is the case with the works of other postcolonial writers already discussed in this chapter, the theme of Nyamnjoh's short stories is translation in literature and its sociological functions in cross-cultural communication. Language-mixing is perhaps one of the most effective strategies of linguistic appropriation at the disposal of this Anglophone Cameroonian writer. It enables him to make the European language bear the burden of an indigenous cultural experience. By inscribing camfranglais words into his text Nyamnjoh succeeds in underscoring the linguistic plurality that has come to characterize creative writing in Cameroon. The juxtaposition of codes in the stories is indicative of the fact that Nyamnjoh's book mirrors real life in Cameroon. It also reveals the fact that Cameroonian writers are able to hold onto their cultural roots by incorporating indigenous linguistic forms into fictional writing in a bid to create a variety of meanings.

In today's multilingual world and increasing globalization cross-cultural communication is inevitable and necessary for survival. As the excerpts above show, the people of Cameroon have already embraced this emerging reality as seen in the infusion of hybrid codes in daily communication. Camfranglais is a hybrid language spoken mostly by teenagers. It is a mixture of French, English and loans from vernacular languages. Kouega defines Camfranglais as: "a composite language consciously developed by secondary school pupils who have in common a number of linguistic codes, namely French, English and a few widespread indigenous languages" (23).

The blending of languages is increasingly becoming a popular mode of creative writing in Caribbean postcolonial literatures. The language employed by Francophone Caribbean fiction writers is a discourse traversed by potent cultural signifiers as seen in the following excerpts culled from Patrick Chamoiseau's seminal novel *Texaco* (1992):

> Je vendis les cocos du pied-coco de Pè-Soltene, un vieux nègre-distillerie qui fumait sa vieillesse sous ce seul arbre planté. Je vendis des crabes que j'allais déterrer sur les terres de Dillon. Je vendis des bouteilles et des casseroles anglaises. Je vendis des fiasques à parfum qu'une pacotilleuse ramenait d'Italie. Ces djobs me procuraient des sous que je serrais comme ceux de Nelta (après avoir payé notre huile, notre sel, notre pétrole, un bout de toile, et cotisé, comme toutes les bonnes gens d'En-ville à la société mutualiste," L'humanité Solidaire (299).

[I sold the coconuts from the tree of Pa Soltene, an old distillery-blackman who smoked away his old-age under his only tree. I sold crabs which I'd dig up on Dillon's lands. I sold bottles and saucepans. I sold perfume flasks that a trinket merchant brought from Italy. These odd jobs brought me money that I (after having paid for the oil, salt, kerosene, a piece of cloth, donated a bit like all of City's good people to the mutual aid society, Human Solidarity) kept like Nelta did] (*Texaco,* 272).

What makes Chamoiseau's narrative style both interesting and intriguing is the fact that he blends together standard French, Martinican regional French, Creole, and his own creative wordplay in order to give esthetic value to his text. He seems determined to invent an original style of writing which critics have dubbed the "chamoisification" of the French language. Chamoisification aptly describes Chamoiseau's linguistic jugglery; his attempt to articulate creole identity in his fictional works. In an interview with Canadian writer, Lise Gauvain[8,] Chamoiseau had the following to say about the issues he has with choosing a style of writing: "Le problème actuel de l'écrivain, c'est justement cette mise en convergence des langues, des valeurs, des peuples, cette diversité qu'il peut désormais exprimer dans son harmonie"(39).[The problem confronting the writer at this point in time is this convergence of languages, values and peoples, this diversity that could be expressed harmoniously.]

Chamoiseau's canonical subversion amounts to a differential discourse that serves as a response to colonial elaboration of authority and forced subjugation. His re-

---

[8] L'écrivain francophone à la croisée des langues (1997)

articulation of Caribbean Francophone identity[9] is visible in the manner in which he blends creolized and metropolitan versions of French in his literary works. The concept of "chamoisification" of French is of special interest to us in this book given that it underscores the novelist's quest for a third code—a personalized writing model quite distinct from that employed by the Metropolitan French writer but also different from the style of his native Creole oral performers. He admits the duality of his writing style in the following words:

> Le rapport que nous devons instituer actuellement, c'est un rapport où, dans l'utilisation de la langue française, nous restons ce que nous sommes: simplement créoles, martiniquais qui, au cours d'un processus historique bien compréhensible, avons intégré cette langue"(37).
> [The kind of relationship that we must have at present, is one where in having recourse to the French langue, we remain who we are: simply Creoles, Martinicans, who in the course of a historical period of time have appropriated this language.]

In Chamoiseau's novels, standard and nonstandard forms of French come together and literally wrestle with each other for control of the narrative, just as they are jostling for power and prestige within the story itself. Commenting on his style of writing in an interview he granted Marie-Jose N'Zenou Tayo, Chamoiseau asserts that it was "… ni un français créolisé, ni un créole francisé, mais un français chamoisisé" (155). […neither creolized French, nor Frenchified Creole,

---

[9]The concept of 'caribbean identity' is well articulated in Edouard Glissant's masterpiece *Le discours antillais*(1981)

but chamoisified French." Readers encountering Chamoiseau's texts for the first time will have to do their homework in order to decipher the significations of the culture-specific tropes the writer employs for the purpose of self-expression. Chamoiseau's language mixing is challenging to read because readers find themselves looking for meanings of words and expressions and stopping to reread unfamiliar sentence structures. The way out of this conundrum is to use the peripheral texts to infer the extended meanings. The use of code-switching in the writer's narrative compounds an initial frustration but over time ideas surface and it becomes comfortable reading. Thus we don't feel so alienated but we are still left contemplating the multiple meanings that are buried in the substructure of the text.

By resorting to this sort of narrative technique, Chamoiseau achieves one of his main objectives, which is to underscore the historical and social complexities that surround language usage in the Caribbean. Translators of *Texaco* did a laudable job of preserving the cultural texture of the source text in the English language translation. Their rendition of the compound noun "Pè-Soltène" as "Pa Soltène" is culturally significant. The word "Pè" is a Creole word derived from the French word "Père". "Pe" is probably a contraction of the French word "Père". The translators did an excellent job of finding a culturally relevant equivalent in the target language. "Pa" appears to be a contraction of the word "Papa". The cultural significance of this translation resides in the fact that Chamoiseau's translators succeeded in conveying the cultural value of the word "Pa" in the target language. In Black communities, this word does not necessarily translate the notion of filial relationship between addresser and addressee. Rather, it is a term of respect used by youths in addressing people of a ripe age. It is a marker of age disparity. Another noteworthy case of indigenization in the text is the writer's use of the word "djobs" in the source text. This word is probably a derivation from the English word "job". It is a transcription of the oral pronunciation of the word "job". Because selling coconuts is not a job in the strict sense of the word, Chamoiseau's translators decided to add the qualifier "odd" which serves as a signifier of socio-economic status in the West Indian context.

In sum, Chamoiseau's hybridized style of writing is a pointer to his inclination toward linguistic indigenization as a form of resistance to French linguistic imperialism. Throughout the narrative the reader feels the writer's unveiled intent to translate Creole language into the French language. His style is syncretic, which bears testimony to the fact that contemporary postcolonial literatures have gone beyond the stage of docile conformity with European models to a stage where writers nurse the urge to deconstruct the language of imperial domination. This process of literary decolonization involves a radical dismantling of European literary frameworks. The deconstructionist enterprise that one notices in the works of Francophone writers takes place in the form of subversion and appropriation of dominant European discourses. Postcolonial literary texts are often constructed in counter-discursive rather than homologous terms. Abrogation and appropriation are manoeuvres that sustain postcolonial writing—a literature that calls into question the validity of the canons upon which colonial literature has been written. Critics of postcolonial literatures maintain that in the history of decolonization, the literary dimension is significant not only because of the themes and preoccupations of literary producers, but also and more profoundly because of their chosen medium (Juneja, 1995; Ngugi, 1986; Olaniyan and Quayson, 2007; Walder, 1998). Postcolonial writers use imposed European languages to write a literature that is entangled not only with their indigenous cultures but also with national histories and identities. Achebe's remarks on the seminal role of language and translation in the literary decolonization process are worth committing to memory:

> The price a world language must be prepared to pay is submission to many kinds of use. The African writer should aim to use English in a way that brings out his message best without altering the language to the extent that its value as a medium of international exchange will be lost. He should aim at fashioning out English which is at once universal and able to carry his peculiar experience….But it will have to be new English, still in full communion with its ancestral home but altered to suit its new African surroundings. (*Morning yet*, 61-62)

Achebe's musings on the need for new Englishes in the excerpt above appears to be an endorsement of the linguistic miscegenation that is being exploited as a new literary canon in contemporary postcolonial literatures. Many postcolonial writers have the conviction that by availing themselves of strategies of appropriation in the creative writing process they are being faithful to their cultures of origin. The tendency to indigenize the colonial language is the expression of a historical process: the Empire imposed a standard metropolitan language on its subjects through its assimilationist system of education; the subjects are now writing back the non-standardized variant of the imperial language which has been usurped, abrogated and appropriated to make it culturally relevant as seen in this example culled from Fouda's text: "Ces temps derniers les jeunes talents se sont vus affubler des substantives "yo" et "yoyettes," surtout s'ils se sont branchés comme des fils électriques, avec pantalons en tire-bouchon...."(62) [Lately, youngsters have begun to refer to each other as "yo" and "yoyettes," especially if they are dressed to the nines and look like electric poles in their corkscrew pants.] The words "jeune" and" talent" though French have been appropriated and endowed with entirely new significations in Fouda's text. In Camfranglais, these two words used together (jeune talents) refer to young girls and boys who are inexperienced in the ways of the world—green horns as it were. "Yo" and "yoyettes" are neologisms created by Camfranglophones to describe young men and women who are fond of dressing up stylishly. The re-shaping of the colonial language to meet the needs of millennia users does not only mark a separation from the site of colonial privilege but also sheds light on the ambivalent nature of postcolonial writing. As Om Juneja points out, "Being heir to two cultures, two languages and hence two worldviews, the colonial writer is trapped in linguistic dualism" (138).

Linguistic dualism or bilingualism offers the postcolonial Cameroonian writer the opportunity to write for a dual readership: Anglophone and francophone as well as local and global. The incontrovertible truth about postcolonial Cameroonian literature is that writers are constantly drawing inspiration from both worlds. In addition to Western literary traditions, Cameroonian writers make use of the oral art forms of diviners, hunters' guilds, rituals and divination as literary motifs. This is true of other fictional works coming out of Africa. A noteworthy illustration of cultural ambivalence in African literature is the final section of *Things Fall Apart* (1958) in which Okonkwo's suicide is reported in such a way that the two opposing views of the white District Commissioner and of Obierika merge into one. The District Commissioner is appalled by the refusal of the tribe to handle Okonkwo's dead body, as he is a "student" of native traditions: "The resolute administrator in him gave way to the student of primitive customs" (164). This phrase makes readers aware of the fact that what they have been reading is English that has been given an African coloration as Obierika's furious outburst indicates: "That man was one of the greatest men in Umuofia. You drove him to kill himself; and now he will be buried like a dog" (165). Achebe's novel is, indeed, an ethno graphic text[10] based on Igbo culture. It is a text where acculturation is a two-way traffic: the Igbo people learn the ways of the white man; the white Commissioner gets acquainted with the customs of the Igbo.

The effective use of proverbs constitutes an integral part of the didactic project in the novel as seen in this example culled from *Arrow of God*: "...but a toad does not run in the daytime unless something is after it" (254-5). The rhetorical value of this wise saying is evident. As Achebe points out, "Among the Ibo the art of conversation is regarded very highly, and proverbs are the palm oil with which words are eaten" (*Things Fall Apart*, 4-5). He makes abundant use of proverbial expressions in order to translate Igbo oral traditions into English. A proverb which is repeated several times in *Arrow of God* is: "A man who brings home ant-

---

[10]An ethnographic text is one that explores the cultural phenomena of a group of people. Ethno texts are often based on the writer's personal experience.

infested faggots should not complain if he is visited by lizards" (59). This sagacious saying serves as an allusion to the European conquest of Africa. Ezeulu first uses this proverb when talking to his wife, after it had been discovered that Oduche had tried to kill a python by shutting it up in a box. Oduche's Christian education accountable for the planned blasphemy is perceived by Ezeulu as a by-product of colonialism. Achebe brings an original voice to African literature written in a European language by closing the gap between the worlds of the colonizer and the colonized through the translation of Igbo culture and worldview into the English language. Fonkou achieves the same goal in his novel as seen in his use of the following proverb: "Les loups ne se mangent pas entre eux" (14). [Wolves do prey on one another.] Recourse to this aphorism associated with the canine world enables the writer to translate the worldview of his people into the French language.

One seminal role of translation as a narrative technique in postcolonial literatures is the elucidatory function it fulfills. Translation serves as a means of explicating some indigenous cultural phenomena in European languages. Kole Omotoso attains this objective in his novel *Combat* (1972) by availing himself of the literary trope of translation in a bid to create fresh idioms in the English language. For example, in the sentence, "Their faces seemed to burst into smiles" (34), "burst into smiles" is a translation from the writer's Yoruba native tongue. In standardized English, this idiom has equivalents such as "wide grins," "broad smiles," or, if "burst" must be used, "burst into laughter." By turning to Yoruba speech patterns, Omotoso adds one more idiom to the English language by translating his Yoruba imagination and speech mannerisms into this European language.

Idiomatic expressions derived from indigenous languages bring along with them a specific perspective of the world which enriches the European language. Moreover, translation in literature conveys semiotic significations on account of the cultural specificity of the metaphors, proverbs, idioms and other rhetorical devices employed by African writers.

This notwithstanding, some scholars of postcolonial literatures argue that translating from indigenous into European languages may be risky business (Griffiths, 1978; Nkosi, 1981; Ojo-Ade 1989; Oluwole, 1998). These theorists posit that even in the hands of skilful writers the undertaking may prove treacherous, the more so because by writing in European languages, postcolonial writers operate outside the boundaries of both their native tongues and those of their adopted languages. In other words, they operate on the fringe of both languages. As Nkosi observes, "Clearly what the African writer lacks in his enterprise is the silent complicity of his people, the majority of whom still use African languages to express their most intimate thoughts and emotions..." (6). However, this dilemma may actually be beneficial given that it imposes on the committed creative writer the sort of mental discipline that is needed to produce outstanding works of literature. Writers' search for appropriate form, their yearning for the sort of distillation of language that would aptly reflect their worldview and cultural specificities often results in the production of the exceptionally well written literary texts that we have at our disposal today.

Critics of postcolonial African literatures often mistake this conscious literary undertaking for linguistic deficiency on the part of writers. Homi Bhabha, for example, argues that "What has been cogitated in one language can never be repeated in the same way in another" (232). Bhabha's remarks should be taken with some reservation because translation in literature goes beyond the replacement of textual material in the indigenous language with equivalent textual material in the target European language. His work on postcolonial theory has come under strong criticism for being overly ambiguous both in its expression and meaning[11]. Intercultural communication cannot be reduced to the mere replacement of lexical items; it involves the deployment of an entire pool of resources at the disposal of the creative writer. Translation in literature involves the transposition of the raw materials of a given language (vocabulary and syntax, as well as the repertory of myths, proverbs, songs, rituals and folklore), to the processing tools (formal and structural devices, such as repetition, typology of address, tropes of arrangement), to considerations of narrative reception (audience and feedback). The truth about postcolonial writers' use of language is that they display a certain degree of ingenuity at linguistic miscegenation. By adapting native tongue syntax and lexical items to European language syntax and lexes, and by situating their texts in culture-specific contexts, these writers exploit the potentials of both indigenous and European languages to produce hybrid texts. An important dimension of postcolonial African literature is the deliberate attempt by writers to not only preserve indigenous cultures in their works but also to shed light on the plurality of voices in the societies they describe.

In an interview he granted this author, Nganang made the following remark about the ramifications of linguistic plurality in postcolonial Cameroonian writing: "Back in the nineties as well as now, there is a strong need to have the broad

---

[11] See Ato Quayson's discussion of Bhahba in *Postcolonialism: Theory, Practice or Process?* (2000)

spectrum of our voices heard. My literature is an attempt to translate this need into writing" (*JALA* 3.2, 209). In the same vein, Achebe makes a conscious effort to translate Igbo speech mannerisms into written English as illustrated in the following passage in *Arrow of God*:

> I want one of my sons to join these people and be my eyes there. If there is nothing in it you will come back. But if there is something there you will bring home my share. The world is like a mask, dancing. If you want to see it well you do not stand in one place. My spirit tells me that those who do not befriend the white man today will be saying had we known tomorrow (20).

This passage reflects Igbo thought patterns. Achebe's recourse to the African mask as a trope is significant given that he likens the activities of human beings to the performance of the masquerade—an element of Igbo oral traditions. Achebe's world is one where parts of the human body are used metonymically to represent the whole. Ezeulu uses the expression, "be my eyes there" to mean "represent me there". Like most African writers, Achebe translates indigenous worldview into the English language. In his writing, English has been domesticated and made to bear the imprint of Igbo culture. Hooks maintains that Achebe "puts together words in such a way that the colonizer had to rethink the meaning of the English language" (Quoted in Dingwaney and Maier, 1995, 297). Fonkou embarks on a similar trajectory by indigenizing the French language as the following sentence from *Moi taximan* shows: "La journée d'hier a été djidja" (19) [Yesterday was djidja.] The word "djidja" used by Francophone and Anglophone

Cameroonians translates the notion of insurmountable difficulty. Cameroonian writers like all African writers attempt to formulate indigenous modes of discourse as a viable means of expressing self-identity (Ashcroft et al., 1989; Chinweizu et al., 1983; Slemon 1994). Texts, more than any other social products, are the most powerful purveyors of cultural identity. Postcolonial Cameroonian writers are particularly preoccupied with the power that resides in textual discourses.

By recasting postcoloniality as a literary discourse, critics implicitly privilege the role of literature in the decolonizing process. The paradigmatic moment of anti-colonial counter-textuality is seen to begin with the deliberate mixing of Western genres with indigenous language tropes and content. Kourouma does this by malinkelizing[12] French. In so doing, he exemplifies the syncretism favoured by postcolonial literary theory. Critics of postcolonial literatures contend that because of the quintessential hybridity of the postcolonial text, it is not possible for writers to return to an absolute pre-colonial cultural purity, nor is it possible for these writers to write fiction that is entirely independent of implication in the colonial discourse (Ashcroft et al., 1989; Jameson, 1986; Khatibi, 1983; Quayson, 2000). This remark is pertinent given the emphasis on cultural dualism in this book. Postcolonial writers seem to be perpetually adrift between two languages and cultures, vacillating from one to the other and subject to indecisiveness. Positioned on the threshold of two 'adversarial' cultures, postcolonial literatures open up an in-between (third) space of cultural ambivalence. In this vein, the writer becomes the bearer of a split consciousness and a

---

[12]For more on this subject matter read Vakunta's *Indigenization of Language in the African Francophone Novel: A New Literary Canon* (2010)

double vision. Apart from the 'impurity' of their language, postcolonial writers suffer from a cultural alienation of sorts. Arguing along the same lines Gandhi maintains that "... the syncretic narrative celebrated by postcolonial critics becomes a distorting mirror in which the anti-colonial nation is forced to recognize its own estrangement" (198). Said is equally vocal in his observations on the subversive nature of postcolonial writing which he describes as transgressing the confinement of both imperial and provincial orthodoxies. As he puts it:

> The authoritative, compelling image of Empire... finds its opposite in the renewable, almost sporty discontinuities of intellectual and secular impurities, mixed genres, unexpected combinations of tradition and novelty (406).

The postcolonial writer, Said argues, has the potential to redefine imperial attitudes toward language and thought. In other words, the writer functions as a literary dissident par excellence. In his close reading of postcolonial fiction, Jonathan White argues that the postcolonial novel is the location of revolutionary consciousness in a world devoid of political and historical content. Although it is hard to believe that the post-colony is a world bereft of political and historical content, there is logic in White's perception of postcolonial prose fiction as a locus of counter-discourse. In his novel titled *Aux Etats-Unis d'Afrique* (2006), Abdourhman Waberi employs the technique of counter-discourse effectively in an attempt to turn the tables as seen in the following passage:

Mais revenons à la cahute de notre pouilleux charpentier germanique ou alémanique....Ce quidam, pauvre comme Job sur son fumier, n'a jamais vu la couleur d'un savon, n'imagine pas la saveur d'un yaourt, ne soupçonne point la douceur d'une salade de fruits. Il est à mille lieues de notre confort sahelien le plus courant (14).

[But let us return to the shack of our flea-ridden Germanic or Alemanic carpenter.... This individual, poor as Job on his dung heap, has never seen a trace of soap, cannot imagine the flavor of yogurt, has no conception of the sweetness of a fruit salad. He is a thousand miles from our most basic Sahelian conveniences] (*In the United States of Africa*, 4.]

In this novel, Waberi uses reverse psychology as both a theme and stylistic device. He reverses the current world order to bring up issues of inequality and biases. By flipping the economic and social powers this way he definitely makes the reader rethink the way the world is and why those who are in power behave the way they do. This novel offers an important criticism of the elitist society that we are so accustomed to. Waberi turns the tables and discusses current problems of Africa as if they were the problems of the rest of the world, especially those in the West. What can be a better way to alert people of your problems then putting them in your position? Waberi's goal is to take readers, especially Western readers, out of their comfort zones. The thought of the existence of a United States of Africa makes the Western reader uncomfortable.

In the same line of thought, White suggests that we have to think of literature as an alternative way of re-writing the status quo. In his collection of essays titled *Recasting the World:*

Writing after Colonialism (1993), White professes his overarching concern about the norms of recasting colonial realities through writing. He locates in the postcolonial text the potential to both cope with the 'terrors' of the colonial aftermath, and the dogmatism that may stall attempts at engendering an improved ethno-political future. In *The Empire Writes Back* one encounters the following dogmatic remarks: "All postcolonial literatures are cross-cultural" (39); "The postcolonial text is always a complex and hybridized formation" (110); "Colonialism inevitably leads to a hybridization of cultures" (129); "Hybridity is the primary characteristic of all postcolonial societies whatever their source" (185). While it is tenable to argue that hybridity is a feature of postcolonial societies and the literatures emerging thereof, it is disheartening to notice that the discourse contained in *The Empire Writes Back* is dangerously prescriptive. Above all, its rigid directives and injunctions exhibit the same canonical rigidity targeted by postcolonial writing. Although the syncretic use of language is an integral part of postcolonial literatures, this does not make all postcolonial texts cross-cultural as purported by Ashcroft, Griffiths, and Tiffin. Certainly there are writers in the postcolonies who harbor no desire at all to translate their indigenous cultures into fictional writing in European languages by having recourse to the technique of indigenization.

Indigenization as an expression of linguistic variance is an important characteristic of postcolonial literatures; but it should be noted that the encounter between indigenous and European cultures may, in the first instance, amount to a confrontation between two heterogeneous sensibilities conditioned by their intrinsic value systems. As Dingwaney points out, resistance in literature may be defined as 'forms of cultural/textual practice(s) by subordinate [i.e., formerly colonized) groups [and individuals] ...contesting the hegemony of their former colonizers, Britain, in particular, and Europe, in general" (2). Our definition of culture is similar to that of Ngugi wa Thiong'o who maintains:

> Culture, in its broadest sense, is a way of life fashioned by a people in their collective endeavour to live and come to terms with their total environment. It is the sum of their art, their science and all their social institutions, including their system of beliefs and rituals (*Homecoming*, 4).

The culture of a people, as expressed in literature, is the way they live; the totality of their beliefs, codes of conduct, all elements that are needed for existence and survival in social settings. It is the totality of the material and spiritual values created by a society in the course of history. Culture embodies all the manifestations peculiar to the community that uses a particular language as its means of expression. In this light, the translation of cultures from one literary medium to another ought not to be a frivolous event; rather it should be informed by the cultural functions of translation. This approach to literary translation calls for a sustained effort on the part of the writer given that translation mediates between two linguistic systems embedded in two different cultures.

Postcolonial writers attempt to blend cultural systems for the purpose of creating something new. This is especially reflected in their use of metaphor, myth and other rhetorical devices such as metonymy, synecdoche and simile. The story, though written, has as narrator a master storyteller, a spell-binding raconteur whose delivery conforms to the styles of traditional storytelling. Such narratives sometimes incorporate some of the dramatic performance dimensions of traditional African storytelling, especially its familiar rhetorical devices. These devices do not only improve the narrative style but also conveys a spirit of resistance to canonical prescriptions. Chinweizu, Jemie, and Ihechukwu posit:

> Thus, some central concern of experimentation for the decolonization of our prose and poetic techniques would be the continuation of traditional forms with a pouring of new wine into old bottles, as it were; the incorporation of these forms as elements in novels, poems and short stories; the employment of traditional devices in saturating quantities that will impart an African tone to the product; and the development out of all these new forms and techniques suitable for rendering of new aspects of contemporary African reality (261).

Linguistic appropriation in postcolonial African literatures resides in incorporating traditional rhetorical devices in European language writing. This implies that if the flavor of African culture is to be retained in the prose narratives written in European languages, these languages have to be flexed to allow for the effective use of indigenous discursive elements. Several African writers have experimented with language to various degrees of success. To date, Kourouma is perhaps the most successful experimenter in French as Achebe is in English. The new generation has produced seasoned linguistic jugglers like Nganang, Fonkou, Fouda and Waberi to name only a few. If the stylistic features of African oral narratives are to be captured in written African literatures, it behoves these writers to ensure that the full range of linguistic resources of oral traditions are rendered in such a manner that the cultural esthetics of African traditions come out in European-language writing in Africa. As Achebe contends:

> The good orator calls to his aid the legends, folk-lore, proverbs...of his people; they are some of the raw material with which he works....One hopes that African writers will make use of them [proverbs] in dialogue, for which they were originally intended(Achebe 1964, vii-viii).

Beside English-speaking writers like Tutuola, Achebe and Okara who have succeeded in incorporating oral material into their prose narratives, attention should be drawn to Francophone writers who have been successful in resuscitating in the written word various genres of African verbal arts. Among them is Yambo Ouologuem with his historical epic *Le Devoir de violence* (1968); Cheikh Hamidou Kane whose *L'aventure ambiguë* (1961) is a portrait of African cultures shaped in the fundamental metaphysical and political premises by the single-voice of the Quran; Ferdinand Oyono with his social satires in *Une vie de boy* (1956) and *Le Vieux nègre et la médaille* (1956). Oyono makes it clear that the diary of his protagonist Toundi Ondoua in *Une vie de boy* is a translation from Ewondo into French:

> C'est ainsi que je connus le journal de Toundi. Il était écrit en ewondo, l'une des langues les plus parlées au Cameroun. Je me suis efforcé d'en rendre la richesse sans trahir le récit dans la traduction que j'en fis et qu'on va lire (*Une vie de boy*, 14).

[That was how I came to read Toundi's diary. It was written in Ewondo which is one of the main languages of the Cameroons. In the translation which I have made and which you are about to read, I have tried to keep the richness of the original language without letting it get in the way of the story itself] (*Houseboy*, 5).

In *Le Vieux nègre et la médaille* Mama Titi represents resistance and resilience against colonial oppression. She defies colonial laws by brewing and selling arki, a local gin outlawed by the colonial administration. By supporting Mama Titi and consuming the alcohol she brews, the men who come to drink in her tavern subvert the control that missionaries and colonial administrators attempted to exert on them. Oyono uses these characters to demonstrate the resilience of the colonized. This self-awareness serves as a precursor to the eventual decolonization movement that was destined to come. The protagonist, Meka is a symbol of cultural hybridity in this novel. His cultural ambivalence is seen to be complete when he buys shoes and a zazou jacket in preparation for the medal award ceremony. Rather than dress in traditional garb he opts for Western-style gear to show to what extent he has been brainwashed to believe in the fallacy of white supremacy.

Ousmane Sembene's narrative in *Les bouts de bois de Dieu* (1962) deserves special mention in this book considering that it is the most successful to date in the corpus of African novels devoted to the depiction of African experience in the colonial and postcolonial eras. These Francophone writers have come to the realization that to transpose African esthetics into literature written in European languages, the writer has to resort to intralingual translation. Creative use of language plays a crucial role in this endeavour. The perspectives inherent in language use itself reveal the magnitude of problems encountered by postcolonial African writers in their quest for literary originality. Working within the oral tradition enables African writers to inscribe descriptive oral narratives into the written word. Tutuola, for instance, makes abundant use of this literary device in the *The Palm-Wine Drinkard*. For example, after the protagonist and his wife leave Faithful-Mother, he says:

> But as we were travelling along in the bush we met a young lady who was coming towards us, but as we saw her coming, we bent to another way, but she bent to the place too, then we stopped for her to come and do anything she wanted to do, because we had sold our "death" and we could not die again, but we feared her because we did not sell our "fear" (72).

Apart from the Africanized usage of the English word "bend" (which could be translated as "take a different direction"), it is obvious that Tutuola intends to make a comment on the use of words such as "death" and "fear." The notion of "selling" one's death is a Yoruba idiomatic expression which translates the despondent state of mind in which the narrator and his wife found themselves when confronted by the ghostly woman. Similarly "selling" their fear could be translated as "mustering courage." Unfortunately, the narrator and his wife did not sell their fear, and this accounts for their state of paranoia. There is more to Tutuola's prose narrative than experimentation with the English language. His fiction depicts the mindset of his people. In this perspective, it stands to reason that, like other

African writers, Tutuola is not only a word-smith but also a purveyor of cultures. His writing constitutes a strong voice in the movement toward the de-Europeanization of African literatures as seen in his bold attempt to take possession of the language of the ex-colonizer. Cognizant of the role of the African writer in the decolonization process, Ngugi wa Thiong'o observes:

> We writers and critics of African literature should form an essential intellectual part of the anti-imperialist cultural army of African peoples for total economic and political liberation from imperialism and foreign domination (*Writers in Politics*, 31).

In this introductory chapter we have attempted to outline the theoretical foundations of postcolonial African literature and sought to establish points of convergence between post-coloniality and the theorizing of postcolonial fictional writing. We have suggested that the study of literature in the postcolonial context has the potential to offer radical insights into the various discursive paradigms used by writers from previously colonized nations in an attempt to articulate cultural otherness. In re-visiting some seminal texts from Africa, the Caribbean, Australia and India, we have identified a key theme underlying postcolonial creative writing: regardless of whether they are written in diglossic or polyglossic contexts, postcolonial writers nurse the desire to appropriate and domesticate the European languages in which they write.

Secondly, our analysis of the interface between orality and literacy, notably arguments concerning the interconnection between indigenous oral and modernist literary traditions have led to a dialogue on the theories of syncretism and hybridity that draw upon both traditions. The examples discussed above indicate that postcolonial writers employ a variety of strategies, including vernacular transcription, pidginization, syntactic fusion, calques, code-switching and loan translations in a bid to not only indigenize their writing but also to deconstruct the prescriptive precepts inherent in European languages.

It is important to note that there are differences between syntactic fusion, calques and code-switching. While syntactic fusion deals with the merging of elements of syntax in a language, especially morphemes, usually accompanied by a change in the form of the elements, a calque refers to a loan translation, especially one resulting from bilingual interference in which the internal structure of a borrowed word or phrase is maintained but its morphemes are replaced by those of the native language. Code-switching, on the other hand, is the alternate use of two or more languages or varieties of a language within the same discourse. These literary devices constitute deliberate attempts by African writers to imprint their worldviews and imagination on European-language texts. Through these perspectives, we may see the positive potential of translation in literature. As suggested in this chapter domestication of language in postcolonial literatures is not exclusively contestatory or oppositional; rather it is writing with colonial antecedents in complex gestures of resistance and de-identification. In this case, domestication is not inevitably a contest, but rather an imaginative site of resistance and transformation that ultimately demonstrates a form of decolonization. At the same time, postcolonial literary theories underscore the dilemmas faced by creative writers in their enterprise to reconstruct national identities through the medium of literature. Literary indigenization enables these writers to translate their experiences and sensibilities into European languages by creating an interface between oral and literary traditions as will be illustrated in subsequent chapters of this book. In Chapter Two, we dwell on code-switching, the alternate use of two or more languages within the same discourse that has occasioned the emergence of a new Cameroonian language code-named *Camfranlais*.

Chapter 2

Camfranglais: The Making of a New Language in Cameroon

Kouega's seminal work, *Camfranglais, A Glossary of Common Words, Phrases and Usages* (2013) is a succinct study of the emergence and structure of Camfranglais. The book has two parts. Part One sheds light on the sociolinguistic and morphological structures of Camfranglais. In Part Two, the author provides readers with a lexical inventory of words and expressions that have come to be considered the functional vocabulary of Camfranglais speakers. Readers who have little or no acquaintance with the Republic of Cameroon many wonder what gave birth to this new urban slang. Kouega notes that Camfranglais was purposefully developed by secondary school students in a bid to freely communicate among themselves to the exclusion of non-initiates. Mbangwana observes that recourse to Camfranglais is triggered by the need for these youngsters to "veil many of their likes and dislikes, many of their ambitions and fears (quoted in Kouega, 2013, p. 9). The origin of the term 'Camfranglais' is attributed to Professor Ze Amvela who commented in the foot-notes of a paper he presented in 1989 as follows: "'Camfranglais' is used here as a cover term to describe what has been called 'Franglais', 'Pidgin French', 'Majunga Talk', 'Camspeak'" (quoted in Kouega, 2013, p.17).

The composite nature of Camfranglais stems from the fact that Cameroon is an ex-colony of France and Great Britain. Official bilingualism (English and French) is, therefore, one of the legacies bequeathed by these ex-colonial powers. Over and above, 248 indigenous languages co-exist with these European languages. Camfranglais is an enigmatic hotchpotch developed from the linguistic plurality that distinguishes Cameroon from other postcolonial nation-states. To the older generation of Cameroonians, Camfranglais remains a mind-boggling linguistic conundrum whose evolution has to be watched closely.

Speakers of Camfranglais make a deliberate attempt to disguise the messages they convey in a speech act as seen in the excerpt below: "Il y a la galère au Camer au day" [There is poverty in Cameroon these days] (155). It should be noted that the word "Camer" sometimes spelled "Kamer" refers to the Republic of Cameroon. It is derived through the process of clipping or truncation. In a similar vein, the expression "au day" is a hybrid word resulting from the combination of the first syllable of the French word 'aujourd'hui' (today)and the second syllable of the English word 'today'. 'Au day' is a neologism obtained by replacing the "jourd'hui" segment of the word "aujourd'hui" with the English word "day." "Galère" is a French word that signifies "hassle" or "trouble." Nonetheless, in the speech of Camfranglones, this word has undergone a semantic shift. It connotes the notion of "poverty." Semantic shifts can be very obfuscating as seen in the following statement: "Ma friend se call Suzy, elle me helep bad" (154) [My friend's name is Suzie; she helps me a lot]. It is interesting to note that the English word 'bad' conveys a positive undertone in the speech of speakers of Camfranglais: 'helep bad' is translated as 'helps me a lot.' It should be noted that 'helep' comes from the English word 'help.'

Camfranglais lexicon is populated by Pidgin English words and expressions as evident in the following excerpt:

"Elle do the buyam-sellam depuis quand?" How long has she been buyam-sellam?] (152) The compound noun 'buyam-sellam' is derived from two English words 'buy' and 'sell.' The term is used in reference to someone who retails foodstuff. Retail trade has greatly enriched the lexicon of Camfranglais as seen below: "J'ai des aff à placer" [I have some items to sell] (122). Notice the clipping process by means of which the word 'aff' is obtained. 'Aff' is an abbreviation for 'affaire'(stuff).

Oftentimes, speakers of Camfranglais resort to code-switching out of a desire to create humor as is noticeable in the following statement: "Il est tellement pressé qu'il a put son calékoum à l'envers= He is in such a hurry that he put on his underwear inside out" (154). The word 'Calékoum' is a camerooniansim for the French word *'caleçon'* [pant or underwear]. The code-switching[13] in this statement is evident. Omole maintains that code-switching "refers to the alternate use of two languages, including everything from the introduction of a single unassimilated word up to a complete sentence or more into the context of another language"(58). He further notes that this linguistic usage presupposes a degree of proficiency in two or more languages from which a speaker or writer can switch back and forth. This is precisely what transpires in all discourses in Camfranglais.

As can be seen in these examples, Camfranglais speakers tend to rely on language mixing as a word formative process as this other example seems to suggest: "Ma rese a tcha le

---

[13]In linguistics, *code-switching* occurs when a speaker alternates between two or more languages, or language varieties, in the context of a single conversation. Multilinguals—speakers of more than one language—sometimes use elements of multiple languages when conversing with each other. Thus, code-switching is the use of more than one linguistic variety in a manner consistent with the syntax and phonology of each variety.

bele et elle talk que c'est avec un attaquant" [My sister is pregnant and she says that her partner is a taxi driver assistant] (129).Notice that the word 'attaquant' is a standard French language word that could be translated as 'assailant' or 'attacker.' However, in the excerpt above, the word has been endowed with an entirely new signification, "taxi driver assistant.' Kouega defines the word 'bele' as "unwanted pregnancy" (138) as the following statements suggests: "Le djo-là est fini: sa nga a tcha le bele et elle veut qu'ils move ça et il n'a pas le do" (138-9) [The boy over there is in trouble: his girlfriend is pregnant and she wants them to remove the foetus and he does not have any money.] Many borrowed lexical items are identifiable in this example. 'Djo' is culled from one of the vernacular languages spoken in Cameroon. It refers to 'man', friend' or 'partner.' 'Tcha' has the following semantic equivalents: 'catch someone red-handed,' 'arrest someone,' 'hold,' and 'take someone along with force' (Kouega, 2013, p.158).

The word 'do' , sometimes spelled 'doh' refers to 'money' as used in the following excerpt: "Il m'a give les do que je lui ai ask hier[He gave me the money I asked for yesterday] (181). Notice that words are spelled differently in Camfranglais. The word 'give' is sometimes written 'gif', 'gib', 'gip', or 'gi' (Kouega, p.197). These heteronyms carry the germ of ambiguity for listeners who have not mastered the rudiments of Camfranglais. It is clear from the foregoing that the word 'give' is prone to misspelling and misinterpretation. This lends credibility to the postulation according to which polysemy[14] is part and parcel of Camfranglais semantics as the

---

[14]Polysemy is the capacity for a word or phrase to have multiple related meanings (sememes).It is usually regarded as distinct from

following example suggests: Je suffer ici trop; better je go" [I suffer a lot here; I would rather leave] (140). Notice that the meaning of the word 'better' in this statement is negative as opposed to the signification of the same word in the following statement: "J'étais un peu sick, mais ça va better" (140) [I was sick but I am feeling better now.]

As one would expect, the sex industry has enriched the lexicon of Camfranglais by furnishing speakers with quite a few words and expressions as seen in the following excerpt: "J'ai tchouké la nga-là mais je n'ai pas bien hia moh" [I have made love with that girl but I did not enjoy it] (297). 'Tchouké' comes from the verbal infinitive 'tchouker' also spelled 'chuker' which could be translated as 'to make love'. The lexeme 'hia,' sometimes spelled 'ya' or 'jia' comes from the English language word 'hear.' In this context, it conveys the idea of having a 'feeling'. Hia moh' is to feel good. Hence, 'moh' is synonymous with the Standard English word 'satisfaction' or 'enjoyment' as in: "Il hia moh" [He is satisfied] (240). Another derivative from 'tchouker' is "tchoukeur' which could be translated as 'womanizer' or 'someone who likes to have sexual intercourse just for the pleasure of doing it. 'Tchouker' has a couple of synonyms: 'nioxer' sometimes spelled 'nyoxer' is a crude, vulgar way of referring to love-making; to have sexual intercourse, or have coitus as in "Si tu as le do tu vas la nioxer là-là-là" [If you have money, you will have sex with her right away] (254).

Another synonym for 'nyoxer' is 'comb' as in: "Toi aussi. How tu comb une ngo trois time en un seul day. Tu es became un coq? [You too. How come you make love with a girl three times in a single day? Have you become a

---

homonymy, in which the multiple meanings of a word may be unconnected or unrelated.

cock?](166) 'Nyoxer' is semantically akin to 'bordelle,' a term used by speakers of Camfranglais to describe a prostitute as in "Lock moi ton mop, une bordelle comme ça!" [Lock me your mouth, or shut up, you prostitute!](146) Note that in the example above, Camfranglophones have recourse to metonymy[15] as a word formative process by having the part (prostitute) represent the whole institution (brothel'). Some Camfranglophones prefer the truncated form of the word 'bok' as in: "Mais gars, tu ne vas quand même pas commot une bok! [But my friend, don't tell me that you will go out with a prostitute (145). Other words that reference prostitutes in Camfranglais are 'wolowoss' (316), 'akwara' (123) and 'sotuc' (288), 'maboya'(229), 'sapak'(281) and 'ashawo'(177).

The word 'commot', often spelled 'komot' derives from Pidgin English. It translates into English as 'come out', 'go out' or 'date' as in the following statement: 'Il commot mainant avec une bêtasse de la tri, une nyè nga même' [He now goes out with the foolish girl in Form Four Class, a useless girl for that matter](167). The word 'nga' has its own synonyms, namely 'ngi', 'ngodele', and 'ngo' [=girl]. Certain sex-related expressions are quite comic: "La nga a tcha le bangala de son djo parce qu'il n'a pas gi le do" [The prostitute caught her partner's penis because he did not give her money] (135). 'Bangala' refers to male genital organs or penis. Camfranglophones often use synonyms such as "bic," "engin" and "wangala." Another really comic one is the

---

[15]Metonymy is a figure of speech in which a thing or concept is called not by its own name but rather by the name of something associated in meaning with that thing or concept. Metonymy works by the contiguity (association) between two concepts. For example, "Hollywood" is used as a metonym for the U.S. film industry because of the fame and cultural identity of Hollywood, a district of the city of Los Angeles, California, as the historical center of film studios and film stars.

following: "How tu came au tuyau avec une Sotuc. Elle peut même te lep ici elle go [How come you invite a prostitute to a party. She can abandon you here and take off with someone else] (288). 'SOTUC' stands for Société des Transports Urbains du Cameroun or Cameroon Urban Transport Company. The acronym refers to the defunct urban transportation company which had buses that transported all types of passengers. By analogy, a girl who sleeps around with all kinds of men is referred to as a SOTUC! Literally, it means 'prostitute.' The manner in which these words are formed is well documented by Kouega (pp.47-68) who maintains that "For work on the syntax of Camfranglais to make sense, a comprehensive morpho-syntactic description of Cameroon French and a few relevant Cameroonian languages must have been done"(47). He further notes that Camfranglais words revolve around the following domains: food, drinks, money, sex, physical looks, state of mind, reference to kin and advertisement (47-9). Words are formed in each one of these categories using various techniques. Compounding is one such technique.

Compounding is a noteworthy word formative process in Camfranglais as the following example suggests: "Quand la nga est came, il a commence à do le bep-bep" [When the girl arrived, he started bragging] (139). The compound word 'bep-bep' is a polysemous word as the following usage provides us with a totally different signification of the word: "Le djo de la nga-là est bep-bep; il peut te kick" [The friend of that girl is a stammerer, he may hit you] (139). Another compound word to take note of is hier-hier' which could be translated literally as "yesterday-yesterday." But speakers of Camfranglais use this compound word in reference to an inexperienced worker or 'novice' of sorts as in the following excerpt: "Il a start hier-

hier et il veut déjà give les orders" [He is a novice and he wants to give instructions] (202). Another compound word frequently employed by speakers of Camfranglais is 'hon-hon-hon,' an ideophone[16] which translates as 'bragging' as in "faire le hon-hon-hon" or "do le hon-hon-hon"=to brag, show off, tell lies to win favours. Kouega provides the following example: "Le député a tell dans son speech qu'il va donner le work aux jeunes; ça c'est le hon-hon-hon" [The parliamentarian in his campaign speech said that he will get jobs for the youths; he is telling lies] (203). This ideophone has a communicative intent. Dingemanse (2010) observes that "Ideophones are depictions, that is, they are special in the way they signify their referents"(24).

Physical looks have produced a handful of compound words through the process of repetition or parallelism[17] such as 'djim djim [very big or very large] as illustrated in the following example: "La nga-là est djim djim pourtant sa mater est mingri" [That girl is very big whereas her mother is skinny] (179). Notice that 'mater' is a loan from Latin. It translates as 'mother' (235). The same could be said of the word 'pater', which may be rendered in English as 'father.' Another compound word relating to physical appearance is 'longo-longo' (225). It is a term generally used to depict

---

[16]Ideophones are words that evoke an idea in sound, often a vivid impression of certain sensations or sensory perceptions, e.g. sound, movement, color, shape, or action. Ideophones are found in many of the world's languages. They evoke sensory events, often conveying a sense of repetition or pluralitypresent in the evoked event.

[17]In grammar, parallelism, also known as parallel structure or parallel construction, is a balance within one or more sentences of similar phrases or clauses that have the same grammatical structure. The application of parallelism improves writing style and readability, and is thought to make sentences easier to process. Parallelism is often achieved using antithesis, anaphora, asyndeton, climax, epistrophe, and symploce.

someone who is very tall and usually slim as in the following excerpt: "Il est longo-longo comme ça et il ne play pas le basket?"[He is so tall but he does not play basket-ball?](225)

'Beau-regard' is a compound noun that refers to 'pork' or 'pig' as seen in "Ma terpa a kill notre dernier beau-regard" [My father slaughtered our last pig] (137). Note that 'terpa' in the inverted form of 'pater.' Camfranglais speakers have a predilection for lexical inversion similar to the gimmicks played by speakers of Verlan[18] as seen in 'rese' [sister], reme [mother], repe [father] and refre [brother].Other compound nouns found in the diction of Camfranglais speakers shed light on the demeanor of the referents as in this statement: "Elle est enter dans la maison elle a take l'argent de son pater et elle est go kunai-kunia gi au feyman" [She entered the house, took her father's money, and foolishly handed it over to the swindler] (220).

It should be noted that swindling or trickery, generally referred to as 'feymania,' is common currency in Cameroon. This activity has greatly enriched the diction of speakers of Camfranglais. 'Feyman' for instance, is the Cameroonianism for 'swindler', 'conman' or 'trickster' (189). 'Feywoman' is the female equivalent of feyman [conwoman]. The repetition of words for emphatic purposes is a word formative technique used very often by Camfranglais speakers as seen in this example: "Fais quoi, fais quoi elle a tcha le bele" [No matter what you think, she is pregnant] (187). Notice the repetition

---

[18]*Verlan* is an argot in the French language, featuring inversion of syllables in a word, and is common in slang and youth language. It derives from a long French tradition of transposing syllables of individual words to create slang words. The name *verlan* is an example: it is derived from inverting the sounds of the syllables in *l'envers*.

of the words "fais" and "quoi" in this example. It serves the purpose of emphasis.

Camfranglophones frequently borrow words from Cameroonian indigenous languages as seen in this excerpt: "Tu oses dire que ton djo te love; sans le tobassi il pouvait meme te look?" [You dare say that your boyfriend loves you, without the spell you cast over him, would he have looked at you?](301) 'Tobassi', an indigenous language word, refers to a love potion often used by Cameroonian women to cast spells on their boyfriends, and at times husbands. 'Tobassi' is synonymous with charm, witchcraft or mystical powers. Reference to occultism is common in the parlance of Camfranglophones on account of the people's belief in witchcraft as the following statement illustrates: "Il a toum sa rese au famla" [He has sold his sister in Famla]. Kouega defines the term 'famla' as "witchcraft, sorcery, fetish, evil sect or society, occultism, dangerous ritual practice" (188). He further notes that 'famla' is associated with Bamileke[19] languages. Words akin to 'famla' are 'niongo', 'kong' and 'mukuaye' (188).

Fulfulde, also known as Fulani, a language spoken in the northern regions of Cameroon has provided Camfranglais speakers with loanwords such as 'walai!' This is an interjection that expresses anger. Another Fulani word that recurs in the speech of Camfranglais speakers is "kai," an

---

[19]Bamileke is the name of an ethnic group which is now dominant in Cameroon's West and Northwest Regions. It is part of the Semi-Bantu (or Grassfields Bantu) ethnic group. The Bamileke people are subdivided into several groups, each ruled by a chief. Nonetheless, all of these groups have the same ancestry and share the same history, culture, and languages. The Bamileke speak a number of related languages from the Bantoid branch of the Niger–Congo language family. These languages are closely related.

interjection expressing anger and signalling reprisal and retaliation (Kouega, 212). It is used more commonly by youths from the northern regions of Cameroon [Adamawa, North and Far North].Kouega observes that Fulani "is the language of Muslim Fulbes who conquered the northern part of Cameroon before colonization" (32). Fulfulde is not the only indigenous language that has enriched Camfranglais. The Beti language, a group of a cluster of mutually intelligible languages spoken in Cameroon, Gabon, Equatorial Guinea and Congo, has equally provided Camfranglais speakers with a sizeable number of words. Examples include 'ahkah,' an interjection expressing disgust and rejection. It is generally used by youngsters from the Beti[20] area of Cameroon. Synonymous expressions include: 'Ahti!' Azham! Zamba! These expressions translate as 'Gosh!'(123)

Cameroon is noted as one of the most corrupt nations in the world. By this token, many camfranglais words are related to graft and influence-peddling as seen in this excerpt: "Pour ce job, le gombo c'est how much?"[For this job, the tip is how much?](198)This is the kind of discourse one would hear in offices in cities such as Yaounde, Douala, Bafoussam, etc. between recruiters and potential recruits. Notice that the word 'gombo' also refers to bribery and corruption. 'Gombo' has its derivatives such as 'gombotique,' an adjective qualifying activities relating to corruption] as in: "Il a comot un chiffre gombotique [He gave an amount which included

---

[20]The Beti-Pahuin are a Bantu group of related peoples who inhabit the rain forest regions of Cameroon, Republic of the Congo, Equatorial Guinea, Gabon, and São Tomé and Príncipe. Though they separate themselves into several individual ethnic groups, they all share a common history and culture.Their languages, from the Bantu subgroup of the Niger–Congo language family, are mutually intelligible and are thus sometimes regarded as dialects of a single tongue, called Beti.

his bribe] (198*).* *Gombotiser* is a neologism coined by Cameroonians to describe the crime of 'giving bribes'. Cameroonians sometimes use the term 'choko' also spelled 'tchoko' as a synonym for 'gombotiser' as in "Si tu choko à la porte on te laisse entrer"(162) [If you bribe at the door, they would let you in.] Another corruption-related term that one hears quite often in the speech of Camfranglais speakers is 'mange-mille' as seen in the following excerpt: " J'ai comot le djo-la mais je ne knowais pas qu'il était mange-mille"[I went out with that man but I did not know that he was a policeman](233). 'Mange-mille' is a compound noun derived from two French words: 'manger' (to eat) and 'mille' (thousand). Kouega observes that policemen assigned to regulate traffic on city streets and highways often indulge in extorting money from taxi drivers, and other road-users usually to the tune of one thousand francs CFA (232).

In a nutshell, Kouega's most recent publication is a treasure-trove of linguistic knowledge. The glossary part of the book is a gem. A thousand odd words are listed in alphabetical order and succinctly defined. Each entry comprises an example of the contextual usage of the word referenced. *Camfranglais, A Glossary of Common Words, Phrases and Usages* is written is a language that may defy understanding for the neophyte on account of the verbal jugglery or *signifying* that characterizes the speech patterns and lexical choices of those who speak Camfranglais. Yet, it is a dependable research tool for anyone interested in understanding the genesis of Camfranglais and the socio-linguistic importance of the new language that has seen the light of day in Cameroon. In the Chapter Three, ample light will be shed on the morpho-syntactic structure of Camfranglais and some of the semantic problems that may arise from recourse to Camfranglais in literature.

Chapter 3

The Signifying Monkey: Le Camfranglais, quelle parlure?

The morpho-syntactic structure of Camfranglais is the theme of a seminal book written by André-Marie Nstobé, Edmond Biloa, and George Echu titled *Le camfranglais: quelle parlure? Etude linguistique et sociolinguistique* (2008), a work that defines Camfranglais as an interlanguage.[21] Camfranglais is described by the aforementioned linguists as "une parlure, c'est-à-dire, une manière de s'exprimer particulière à quelqu'un ou à un groupe d'individus"(9) [mumbo jumbo, in other words, a speech mannerism characteristic of a person or group of people][22]. Camfranglais may sound like gobbledygook[23] to the non-initiate on account of the proliferation of double-talk in it. It is described in this book as a composite[24] spoken by young Cameroonians "désireux de s'exprimer entre eux de telle sorte qu'ils ne soient compréhensibles que par les

---

[21]An *interlanguage* is the term used to describe a dynamic linguistic system that has been developed by a learner of a second language (or L2) who has not become fully proficient yet but is approximating the target language: preserving some features of their first language (or L1), or overgeneralizing target language rules in speaking or writing the target language and creating innovations. An interlanguage is idiosyncratically based on the learner's experience with the L2. Interlanguage theory is usually credited to Larry Selinker (1972), who coined terms such as "interlanguage" and "fossilization."

[22] All translations are mind except otherwise indicated.

[23]Languagecharacterizedbycircumlocutionandjargon,usuallyhardtounderstand.

[24]A language made up of several elements drawn from other languages.

locuteurs...capables de décoder les termes empruntés à l'anglais, au pidgin English ou aux langues camerounaises."(9) [intending to express themselves among peers in such a manner that they are understood only by listeners who are capable of decoding terms borrowed from English, Pidgin English or Cameroonian native languages.] The work comprises a preface, six chapters and a conclusion. The preface written by Ntsobé is followed by Echu's introduction in which he sheds ample light on the linguistic configuration of the Republic of Cameroon, especially the linguistic plurality that has engendered creolization and pidginization in this sub-Saharan nation-state.

In Chapter One, Biloa provides a working definition of the term `camfranglais'. In the second chapter, he adumbrates the concept of composite languages, of which Pidgin English and Camfranglais constitute an integral part. The sociolinguistics of Camfranglais is the crux of the discussion in chapter 3 in which Echu analyzes the correlation between Camfranglais and other language usages in Cameroon. In chapter 4, Biloa provides a succinct analysis of the phonology of Camfranglais. Echu delves into an analysis of Camfranglais from point of view of word formative processes in chapter 5. Finally, in chapter 6 Biloa treats readers to an appreciation of the morpho-syntactic structure of Camfranglais. Aside from transcribed oral interviews conducted in academic and non-academic circles in Yaoundé, Douala, Bafoussam and other Cameroonian cities, these researchers had recourse to the mass media (*Cameroon Tribune*), MA theses and Ph.D. dissertations in the crafting of this book.

They contend that the emergence of Camfranglais marks the beginning of a linguistic revolution in Cameroon. As they put it, "le camfranglais s'enrichit et se revitalize de divers apports linguistiques conduisant à une véritable révolution culturelle..." (9)[Camfranglais is enriched and revitalized by means of diverse linguistic borrowings leading to a real cultural revolution]. Camfranglais, they maintain, is tantamount to linguistic invasion that threatens the very survival of the French language spoken in Cameroon: "Il faut admettre, il s'agit bien d'une invasion, d'une dictature de mots et de termes venus d'ailleurs et qui diminuent quotidiennement l'occurrence d'utilisation d'un vocabulaire proprement français" (9)[We must admit that we are actually talking about an invasion, a sort of dictatorship of words and expressions originating from elsewhere which compromises the proper usage of standard French language vocabulary on a daily basis]. To put this differently, the quintessence of Camfranglais is the deconstruction of the sacrosanct grammatical canons of the French language. To this end, camfranglophones tend to resort to a variety of word formative paradigms.

The technique of semantic shift, Ntsobé et al. observe, is a common word formative process in Camfranglais as the following example shows: "Allons book" (22) which could be translated as "Let's go play cards." This two-word sentence could pose serious comprehension problems for non-speakers of Camfranglais. The reason is that the English word "book" has been attributed a new signification for the purpose of linguistic appropriation. As Ntsobé et al. point out, "...des mots issus de l'anglais on été désémantisés et resémantisés, c'est-à-dire qu'ils ont perdu leur sens initial pour en acquérir un autre" (22)[Words originating from English have been divested of their original meanings and endowed with different significations, in other words, they lost their original meanings and acquired new ones.] There is the likelihood of obfuscation for speakers who situate themselves outside the select group of camfranglophones when English words are transposed into the lingo as the following sentence illustrates: "Je vais eat le jazz à la long"(90) [I am going to eat the beans at home]. The word 'jazz' no longer refers to a musical instrument in this context. It has acquired a different meaning "beans." In a similar vein, the word "long" no longer fulfils its English language adjectival function in Camfranglais. Instead, it is used here as a noun, meaning "home," 'house," or "residence." To further complicate matters, camfranglophones sometimes use the same word as a verb as seen in this sentence: "Le djo-ci long dans une villa non loin du lycée"(90) [This guy lives in a villa not far from the high school.] The de-adjectivization of the word "long" constitutes a potential point of ambiguity for listeners who do not speak camfranglais. Similarly, the word "kick" takes on a new meaning in the following sentence: "On a kick mon agogo"(22) [Someone has stolen my wrist watch.] The English word 'kick' loses its original meaning and takes on a new signification 'to steal.' Speakers of Camfranglais seem to have deep love for language mixing and re-appropriation of words. This explains why Ntsobé et al. caution that to decipher the latent significations of English words used in Camfranglais, "Il faut absolument connaître la signification de ces mots dans leurs contextes spécifiques"(90)[One must absolutely be conversant with the meanings of these words in their specific contexts.]

Ntsobé et al. further posit that some lexical items employed by speakers of Camfranglais are loans from Cameroonian vernacular languages as this example shows: "Ne me bring pas ton ndoutou, tu es un poisseux"(106) [Don't bring me bad luck, you're unfortunate.] In

Cameroonian parlance, the word "ndoutou" is worse than 'bad luck'; it is ill-luck that often breeds more incidents of bad-luck. Kouega (2013) notes that this word is sometimes spelled 'ndutu' as seen in the following statement: "Hey gars ne me bring pas le ndutu" [Hey, my friend, you're wishing me ill luck!](250) Linguistic hybridity, the hallmark of Camfranglais, is visible in this sentence. There are two English words 'hey' and 'bring,' a vernacular language word 'ndutu' and the rest is French. 'Ndutu' is borrowed from the Duala language spoken in the Littoral Region of Cameroon. The following example is interesting: "All les gars du kwat-ci sont des ndosses" (106) [All the guys in this neighbourhood are smart.] Kouega (2013) defines 'ndos' as "someone who looks responsible enough in his community, someone intelligent; a boss, a well-to-do person" (249). He provides this example in order to acquaint readers with the contextual usage of the word: "Erreur for mbutuku na damer for ndos"[An idiot's mistake is an asset for an intelligent person] (250). In other words, you have to learn to avoid making mistakes or agree to pay for each one you make. Note that 'kwat', short for quartier (i.e. Neighbourhood) has an orthographical variant, 'quat' as seen in the following statement: "Il y a quoi au quat?"[What is up in the quarter?](271) 'Damer' also 'damé' is the Camfranglais word for 'cooked food.' It is also used as a verb (i.e. to eat).

More often than not, Camfranglophones borrow words from the English language as seen in this statement: "Quand tu look le couple-ci, ils ont l'air très jeune alors qu'ils sont marred depuis from"(109) [When you look at this couple you have the impression that they are young but they have been married for ages.] The expression "depuis from" translates a very long period of time, an unfathomable time span.

Evidently, placing the English preposition "from" in the terminal position as the speaker does above further complicates matters for a listener not familiar with Camfranglais. Ntsobé et al. agree with Kouega that repetition is an important word formative process in Camfranglais as the following example illustrates: "Tu tone-tone quoi? Tu tcha lequel des deux ways ou alors je t'emballe all ça?"(113) [Why are you hesitant? Which one do you prefer? Do you want both?] The compound word "tone tone" comes from Pidgin English. It translates as "hesitate" or "play for time." The words "ways" has nothing to do with the word "way" in Standard English. It refers to "goods" or "shopping items." Kouega (2013) defines the term as "a polysemous word whose meaning can only be deduced from a specific context of usage" (315). He provides the following illustrative examples:

> "Je dois buy les ways pour cook ce soir"= I have to buy some items to cook this evening." In this sentence, "ways" translates as "shopping items."
> "J'ai find le way que j'étais en train de falla"= I have found what I was looking for. In this context, "ways" means "thing."
> "Mon pater est go see ma mater pour le way et elle a gi"=My father discussed that issue with my mother and she accepted. In this excerpt, "ways" is the equivalent of "issue."
> "Ma nga est bele et je n'ai meme pas les do pour buy les way du muna"= My girlfriend is pregnant and I do not even have money to buy baby clothes. In this example, "way" is synonymous with "baby clothes."

It is noteworthy that this is not an exhaustive list of contextual uses of the word "ways" in Camfranglais. The following excerpt is one more example of how compounding is used as a word in Camfranglais: "Sa moto est encore nian-nian" (124) [His car is brand new.] Camfranglophones use the compound word "penia penia" synonymously with "nian-nian," as in "La nga est en haut, son djo a buy une merco penia penia"= the girl is up; her boyfriend has bought a brand new Mercedez car (263). Camfranglais speakers often resort to the expression "être en haut" to express their frustration at the repulsive attitude of civil servants who embezzle state funds. Some repetitions are laden with humorous sexual innuendos as this example shows: "Mola, je go où avec une djim djim mater? (124)[Man, what's my business with such a terribly fat woman?] These compound words sound like ideophones. The prevalence of ideophones in the speech of Camfranglophones is attributable to the fact that Cameroonians tend to translate orality into the spoken word by having recourse to parallelisms. Some of the words repeated are borrowed from Cameroonian native languages. This is the case with a word like "keleng keleng" (80) (edible leaves). Loans fulfil the communicative function of bridging cultural gaps as seen in the use of the Bamileke term "famla" (82) to translate the belief in witchcraft, an essentially African superstitious mindset.

Ntsobé et al. note that Pidgin English has enriched Camfranglais enormously as seen in the following statement: "Je tell que c'est quand tu laï les ngas qu'elles te hia"(118)[I am telling you that girls only believe you when you lie to them.] The word "laï" is a deformation of the English word "lie." As noted above, lexical truncation is common in Camfranglais utterances as seen in this humorous sentence:

"Ton copo là me wanda; on le lap avec ses shoes-là, il ne hia pas"(118) [This friend of yours amazes me; he seems not to care when people make fun of his shoes.] Or this aggressive one: "Je ne fia personne, s'il me touch je le bolè."(120)[I am not afraid of anyone; if he messes with me I'll kill him.] 'Bole' and 'Bolè' are polysemous. It could be translated as: to finish, to end , to die, to run out of, or to be short of money as seen in this statement: "Si tu comot les nga comme ça et tes dos bolè, ne me call pas! [As you are going out with girls at this rate, if you run out of money, don't count on me!](Kouega, 2013, p.145)It is evident from these examples that Camfranglophones take the liberty of toying with English and French, official languages spoken in Cameroon. It is on this count that Ntsobé et al. argue that Camfranglais is a language of resistance against cultural imperialism.

The discourse in *Le camfranglais: quelle parlure? Etude linguistique et sociolinguistique* revolves around the use of neologism as a word formative modus operandi. Neologisms abound in Camfranglais as these examples show: "tchoukeur" (72) [philanderer]; "tchatcheur" (72) [someone who likes to chat up girls]; "jazzeur" (72) [some who is fond of eating beans]; Beignetariat(138)[place where a type of cakes are sold, usually with pap and beans]; obamania(117) [new way of referring to the American Diversity Visa Lottery], parabag(116)[handbag or purse], Amerimania(117)[new way of referring to the American Diversity Visa Lottery] , and au day(129)[today].

Some camfranglais expressions are anagrams or inversions similar to words that one would find in French verlan lexicon: répé (père); rémé (mère); refré ((frère) and résé (soeur) (73). A sizeable number of Camfranglais words are abbreviations as seen in the following examples:

"chem"(Chemise); "merco" (mercedez); "nden" (identification papers); "tako" (taxi); " sofa" (suffer) (85); "bao" (baobab); "copo" (copain); "San con" (sans confiance); "BH" (Beignet-haricot) (97), and "quat" (quartier) (100). As these examples illustrate, the suppression of terminal syllables is a technique constantly employed by Camfranglophones to create new words.

In a nutshell, a reading of *Le camfranglais: quelle parlure? Etude linguistique et sociolinguistique* reminds readers of Gates' book, *The Signifying Monkey: A theory of African-American Literary Criticism* (1989) in which he explores *signification* (or *signifying*) as a literary trope in African American literature. He analyzes the significance of recourse to *signifying* tropes in literary criticism. Gates' theory has served as an impetus for renewed interest in the fictional works of a new generation of French-speaking Cameroonian writers such as Fouda whose rich novel, *Je parle camerounais* (2001), is analysed in Chapter Four.

Chapter 4

Literary Camfranglais in Mercédès Fouda's *Je Parle camerounais: pour un renouveau francofaune*

Those who believe that writers in France's post-colonies write in exactly the same way as mother-tongue metropolitan writers do, would have to rethink after reading Mercédès Fouda's novel titled *Je parle camerounais: pour un renouveau francofaune* (2001). Like fiction writers everywhere within the sphere of *la francophonie*[25], Fouda tries to jettison the yoke of linguistic and cultural imperialism by domesticating the French language in an attempt to convey indigenous thought patterns, speech mannerisms, worldview, imagination and socio-cultural experiences. The debate that revolves around the justification for recourse to the techniques of

---

[25] The Organisation internationale de la Francophonie (OIF), known informally and more commonly as *La Francophonie* is an international organization representing countries and regions where French is the first ("mother") or customary language; and/or where a significant proportion of the population are francophones (French speakers); and/or where there is a notable affiliation with French culture.The organization comprises fifty-seven member states and governments, three associate members and twenty observers. The term *francophonie* also refers to the global community of French-speaking peoples comprising a network of private and public organizations promoting special ties among all Francophones. In a majority of member states, French is not the predominant native language. The prerequisite for admission to the Francophonie is not the degree of French usage in the member countries, but a prevalent presence of French culture and language in the member country's identity, usually stemming from France's colonial ambitions with other nations in its history.

domestication and foreignization as means of literary creativity has attracted the attention of literary critics and translation theorists for a long time. Venuti, for instance, has devoted an entire book *The Translator's Invisibility: A History of Translation* (1995) to the study of these techniques.

It should be noted that *domestication* of language as a literary canon has been used by award-winning fiction writers all over the francophone world. Notable examples are writers such as Henry Lopès (1982), Patrick Chamoiseau (994), Michel Tremblay (1972), Ahmadou Kourouma (1970), Nazi Boni (1962), Patrice Nganang (2001), Gabriel F. Kuitche (2001), and Mercédès Fouda (2001). These writers consciously manipulate the French language in an attempt to reflect specific sociolects[26] and speech patterns while writing in the language of the ex-colonizer. Thus, linguistic experimentation with the language of the ex-colonial masters harbors not just esthetic but also socio-political undertones. When creative writers resort to domestication as a literary device they do so in a bid to superimpose indigenous linguistic tropes and value systems upon the foreign language and culture. By resorting to the domestication of French in *Je parle camerounais* Fouda gives prominence not just to her native tongue but also to the kind of informal French that is spoken by the Cameroonian rank and file as this example shows: "Le 'mamba' alias billet de dix mille francs, de couleur verte, qui

---

26 In sociolinguistics, a sociolect or social dialect is a variety of language (a register) associated with a social group such as a socio-economic class, an ethnic group (precisely termed ethnolect), an age group, etc. Sociolects involve both passive acquisition of particular communicative practices through association with a local community, as well as active learning and choice among speech or writing forms to demonstrate identification with particular groups. Sociolinguists define a sociolect by examining the social distribution of specific linguistic terms.

cause dans les bars autant de dégats que la morsure de son homonyme reptilien sur les humains"(6)[The 'mamba' alias the ten thousand CFA francs green banknote, that causes as much havoc among human beings in bars as the bite of its reptilian counterpart.] By using the word 'mamba' (venomous green snake) to describe money, Fouda underscores the importance of fauna and flora in the speech patterns of Cameroonians. Kouega notes that the word 'mamba' is commonly used by speakers of Camfranglais in reference to "a ten thousand francs bank note" (231). He further observes that in present day Cameroon, this bank note which was greenish in color like a mamba, has changed to violet but the word has survived. In Cameroon, the 10000 CFA bill often arouses feelings of envy when someone takes it out of his or her wallet to buy drinks in a bar. The reason is that it is often perceived by onlookers as a marker of the socio-economic well-being of the spender.

Recourse to words coined to describe Cameroon's flora is evident in this other example: "Le gombo, c'est ce petit job périodique et sporadique dont les revenus disparaissent aussi rapidement que son homonyme, plante mucilagineuse dont on fait les sauces, et qui, surtout cuisinée avec du couscous, descend à toute vitesse dans la gorge"(36)[Gombo is this menial job that one gets occasionally whose revenue disappears as rapidly as its floral homonym, plant used in making soup which descends with ease down the throat, especially when eaten with fufu. Pundits of these kinds of professional acrobatics are called 'gombists.'] It should be noted that Gombo is "okra" but in this context, it is used as an equivalent to the English language word "windfall." However, this word seems to be polysemous in the sense that it is endowed with other significations as this example shows:

"Pour ce job, le gombo, c'est how much? [For this job, the tip is how much?] (Kouega, p.198) The examples above show that the word 'gombo' has undergone semantic shifts depending on the universe of discourse. Arguing in the same vein, Lillian Ndangam (2009) notes that "Within Cameroonian journalism, the term *gombo* is a popular metaphor for various payments, freebies and rewards solicited by journalists and provided by different news actors to journalists. The ultimate aim of giving gombo is to influence what and who is covered, and how they are covered." (819)

Fouda writes back to the Empire in stark defiance of French grammatical conventions. He is insinuating to the ex-colonizers: you taught me French but I am going to domesticate it to the extent where you will have a hard time recognizing your language when you read it in my works. This is what makes her French an 'embargoed' language from the perspective of Metropolitan speakers of French. If the *Académie française* had its way, it would not hesitate to put Fouda's book in a state of pariah on account of her linguistic non-conformity. The quest for linguistic autonomy is evident from the onset—the title of Fouda's book, itself, speaks volumes about the author's linguistic dissent. By titling her novel *Je parle camerounais,* she distances herself from Metropolitan French writers. She does not write: Je parle le français camerounais; rather she writes: 'Je parle camerounais.' Here is another example of Fouda's attempt to appropriate French in her text: "Attifé ainsi, vous seriez ridicule, et Max a bien raison une fois de plus de montrer ses 'attrape-manioc': il se moque gentiment de vous." (37) Les "attrape-manioc" is a reference to human teeth. Because the staple food of Fouda's people is cassava (manioc) she uses this compound word in reference to teeth. 'Attraper le manioc' avec ses dents is to 'eat a meal of cassava'. This usage clearly shows that the French in Fouda's text has been subjected to indigenization (or domestication) to reflect Cameroonian socio-cultural realities. Kouega sheds light on the word 'manioc' by referring to a national Cameroonian dish made of manioc, namely *bâton de manioc*. He provides an example to drive home his point: "Gars, va nous tcha un bâton de manioc dans l'armoire" [Can you get some cassava from the cupboard for us, please!](137) Notice that literally 'bâton de manioc' translates as "stick of cassava." A Westerner reading *Je parle camerounais* is likely to draw a blank on account of the 'foreignness' of Fouda's lexicon. The novelist uses neologisms typical of Cameroonian speech patterns as this example illustrates: "J'ai seulement un 'papa-j'ai grandi' et les 'sans confiance'."(37) Light has been shed on these expressions in a preceding chapter.Kouega provides the following example to show how Cameroonians use the term: "How tu comot dans la boue avec les sans-confiance?" [How come you know the road is muddy and you wear slippers?](281)

Readers of *Je parle camerounais*....may wonder what sort of translation process takes place in Fouda's text. It is worth mentioning that the term 'translation' is not used in this chapter to refer to the replacement of a text in the source language by a lexically and semantically equivalent text in the target language. The translation activity that goes on in this text is intra-lingual.[27] Intra-lingual translation occurs within

---

[27]In an article titled "Intralingual Translation: An Attempt at Description" (META 54.4, 2009)Zethsen provides a terse definition of the term as follows: "Intralingual translation is an interpretation of verbal signs by means of other signs of the same language" (797).

the source language. It is a creative transposition process in which writers attempt to infuse their works with the imprint of their cultural backgrounds, worldview and imagination with the intent of taking control of the language of the ex-colonizer. Fouda transposes the world view of Cameroonians into the French language through the techniques of semantic shift, lexical interpolation, neologisms, reduplication and code-switching.

Code-switching is a technique that Fouda employs with dexterity to fictionalize Cameroonian lived experiences. Her text provides readers with the opportunity to read the type of domesticated French that is spoken in the neighbourhoods and informal spheres in Cameroon. *Je parle camerounais* is replete with Camfranglais, Pidgin English and indigenous language words and expressions that endow the text with a stamp of cultural identity.

Semantic shift enables Fouda to attribute new significations to existing French words as the following example indicates: "En somme, la fête est mondiale, terme exploité quand il y a foule, et que les gens apprécient, comme lors des coupes du monde de foot."(54-55) In Fouda's text, the word "mondial" loses its original signification of "worldwide" and takes on the additional meaning of "extraordinary." She constantly shifts meaning for the purpose of transcribing the speech patterns of her characters into French as this other example seem to illustrate: "Ces temps derniers les jeunes talents se sont vus affubler des substantives "yo" et "yoyettes," surtout s'ils se sont branchés comme des fils électriques, avec pantalons en tire-bouchon..." (62) The words "jeune" and" talent" though French have been indigenized and endowed with entirely new significations in this context. It is worth mentioning that words like "yo" and "yoyettes" are Cameroonian neologisms. Both words describe young boys and girls in Fouda's novel. Kouega provides the following definition for the term 'yo' also spelled 'yoh: "a lad, young boy; a young boy that dresses well" (319). For 'yoyette' he provides this definition "a young lady, a young girl that dresses well" (319). He uses the following example to expatiate: "La yoyette-là a put une belle dress au day" [That young lady is wearing a very beautiful dress today] (319). Linguistic indigenization of the type that one finds in *Je parle camerounais* text has the potential of rendering the novel incomprehensible for a non-Cameroonian readership given that these lexes are culture and context-specific.

More often than not, Fouda resorts to linguistic tricksterism for the purpose of creating humor as the following sentence suggests: "Et puis vous n'aimez pas les papayes, filles à la peau-cratère décolorée tirant sur l'orange, vous préférez le cirage, les noires à la peau luisante" (63) [Besides, you don't like papaya, girls with cratered orange-like complexion; you prefer shoe polish, those with shiny black skin.] The word "papaye" (papaya or pawpaw) is used here to describe an African girl who has made abortive attempts to lighten her complexion by means of body-lightening creams. Such unsuccessful attempts often result in a complexion that is neither black nor white. For want of a better word, Camfranglais speakers generally refer to this kind of complexion as "papaya." In some parts of Cameroon, these girls are said to be suffering from "yellow fever," a derogatory term used to deride their mania for light complexion. Equally hilarious is Fouda's attempt to create a correlation between a woman with huge buttocks and a national debate or conference of sorts on a topic of grave importance as the following sentence shows:

> "De trop larges débats, qui qualifient les gros derrières, et par extension les grosses personnes, puisque si l'on doit discuter en fonction des mensurations, on ne saurait rapidement faire le tour des grosses corpulences"(63)
> [Too big debates, term used to describe big buttocks, and by extension fat people, since it would be an unfeasible task to quickly measure the dimensions of these persons.]

The linguistic manipulation that takes place in Fouda's narrative speaks volumes about the author's conscious attempt to translate orality into the written word; to domesticate the French language for the purpose of expressing a unique worldview, cultural specificity and self-identity. On this topic, literary scholar, Ojo-Ade, makes the following pertinent remarks:

> On the whole, one may safely say that the dual culture of the African writer (the native culture he is writing about and the European culture he has imbibed) makes him first and foremost a translator before being a creative artist ("The Role of the Translator,"295)

One could deduce from Ojo-Ade's observations that the translation of indigenous imagination and worldview into a European language remains a salient feature of contemporary Cameroonian literature of French expression. Thinking along the same lines, Gyasi posits that contemporary fictional writing in Africa is "a creative translation process that leads to the production of a …text in French and the development of an authentic African discourse" (151). Kourouma, for instance, has distinguished himself among Francophone African writers by articulating his views on the type of translation activity that takes place in his fictional writing. In an interview he granted Moncef Badday on the stylistic choices he had to make in *Les soleils des indépendances* (1970), he had this to say:

> J'adapte la langue au rythme narratif africain... Ce livre s'adressse à l'Africain. Je l'ai pensé en malinké et écrit en français prenant une liberté que j'estime naturelle avec la langue classique....Qu'ai-je donc fait? Simplement donné libre cours à mon tempérament en distordant une langue classique trop rigide pour que ma pensée s'y meuve. J'ai donc traduit le malinké en français en cassant le français pour trouver et restituer le rythme africain. (38)
> [I adapt my language to the African narrative style....This book is addressed to the African reader. I thought in Malinke and wrote in French, taking some liberty I consider natural with the classical language .... So what did I do? I simply let go my temperament by distorting a classical language otherwise too rigid to enable my thoughts to flow freely. I, therefore, translated Malinke into French, breaking the French to find and restore the African rhythm].

There is no gainsaying the fact that an understanding of the contextual use of Cameroonianisms used in Fouda's *Je parle camerounais* would serve to enlarge readers' comprehension of the text and make it more accessible than it would be if they were to learn nothing of the circumstances surrounding its creation. Fouda often spices her text with expressions that may be comprehensible only to the closed circle of Camfranglais speakers: "Si depuis belle lurette vous vous démenez de-ci de-là sans trouver aucune occasion à saisir sur le plan matériel, vous pourrez toujours vous plaindre que le dehors est dur..." (5). [If you have been searching here and there in vain for a job to make ends meet, you could always complain that times are hard.] "Le dehors est dur" is a Cameroonianism[28] that conveys the idea that times are hard. This interesting one would certainly intrigue readers not familiar with Camfranglais: "Bon, on fait comme ça! Dira-t-on en guise d'au revoir" (8) [Alright, let's do it that way! One would say as a gesture of taking leave.] The expression "On fait comme ça!" is meant to translate the standard French expression "Au revoir" [goodbye]; "A tout à l'heure" [see you soon] or "A bientôt" [see you later]. This sort of writing certainly puts the burden of translating Cameroonian's socio-linguistic realities to the world on the critic who must then be a Camfranglais cultural insider. Interestingly, this aspect of African literature remains unexplored by those who have a stake in African creative writing, thus leaving the reader to surmise the rationale behind this constant recourse to translation in fictional writing. Arguing along the same lines, Ezekiel Mphahlele observes:

> The major problem facing the African writer is the problem of explaining and translating Africa to the modern world, to Europe, to the world of culture .... The African writer who writes in English or French is interested in seeing that French and English cultures recognize what he and his culture are. It is for this reason

---
[28]Speech patterns and discursive mannerism typical of Cameroonians

that he tries to be the translator of his culture (Quoted in Egejuru, 116)

Fouda translates Cameroonian discursive particularisms into French by employing indigenous language idiomatic expressions as seen in this statement: "Et puis, vous haussez les épaules, il crache je mange? Il pisse je bois?"(62) Literally, these idioms could be translated as: Do I eat his spittle? Do I drink his urine?" These statements translate the contempt the speaker has for the person referenced. A metropolitan speaker of French is likely to say, "Je me moque de lui" or 'Je m'en fou comme de l'an quarante." Similarly, when the narrator says: "Ce dernier, qui ne parle non plus avec l'eau dans la bouche, veut vous rallier à son opinion: fuir le plus rapidement possible" (67), he is translating native tongue parlance into the French language. The expression "parler avec l'eau dans la bouche" could be written in standard French as "tenir des propos incongrus or mensongers" which could be translated as "to tell lies or tall tales." Zabus describes this mode of creative writing as "the writer's attempt at textualizing linguistic differentiation and conveying African concepts, thought patterns and linguistic concepts through the ex-colonizer's language" (23).

Fouda constantly spices her texts with Camfranglais words and expressions that may be comprehensible only to Cameroonians because they are words created by Cameroonians in a multilinguistic communication context as seen in the following statement: "votre estomac vous lance des insultes" (9).Euphemisms are part and parcel of Fouda's lexicon. When a Francophone Camfranglais speaker says, "mon estomac me lance des insultes," she or he is saying that s/he is hungry. In a similar vein, Cameroonians use the expression, "manger son midi" (9) to translate the standard French expression "manger son déjeuner"[eat one's lunch],le midi being the name given to any meal eaten between noon and 2: 00pm. It is important to know that such meals are generally not eaten at home. Rather, they are eaten in makeshift open-air restaurants erected on sidewalks as this statement makes explicit: "Vous avez alors la possibilité d'aller manger au tournedos. Ne vous réjouissez pas trop vite! Vous n'irez que dans l'un de ces restaurants de plein air, faits de bancs et de tables assemblés, et ou, tout bêtement, le client tourne le dos à la route!"(10)[You now have the opportunity to go eat in a *turn-back* restaurant. Don't be too excited! You will go to one of these makeshift restaurants in the open air, where benches and tables are assembled for clients to sit and sheepishly turn their backs to the street!] Notice that the word 'tourne-dos' has no equivalent in standard French because this cultural reality does not exist in France. Thus, context is of the essence for non-Cameroonians reading Fouda's novel.

Fouda's text is filled with compound words created from the different vernacular languages spoken in Cameroon. Examples include: "Mamie Koki" (10), "mamie ndolè" (10), "mamie atchomo" (10) etc. The word "mamie" is the Pidgin equivalent of the standard French "mère." Cameroonian youths generally address older women as "mamie" as a gesture of respect. In the commercial arena, this term is used as a reference to a woman from whom one buys food on a regular basis as the following excerpt shows: "Au tournedos, officie l'asso, diminutive flatteur de "associé (e),est cette personne chez qui vous faites régulièrement des achats et qui, lorsque c'est fort sur vous, vous fait manger un crédit..."(10) It should be noted that "manger un crédit" is a typical cameroonianism that translates the standard expression "acheter à credit"(to buy on credit). It is evident that the word "manger" has been given a different signification in this context. "Manger" could be translated as "acheter." The expression "c'est fort sur vous' translates the standard French expression "les temps sont durs," which could be translated as "times are hard." "Koki," "Ndolè," and "atchomo" are local Cameroonian dishes that carry lots of cultural significations.

In a nutshell, Fouda's *Je parle camerounais: pour un renouveau francofaune* is an indigenized ethnographic novel that seems to defy comprehension on account of the peculiarity of the French language in which it is written. Fouda has tinkered with Molière's language to the point where it is almost unrecognizable by native speakers of French. Teaching this novel places an enormous burden on the instructor and students—the strain of interpretation and elucidation. So why teach it? I decided to include this novel on the list of required readings for my upper-level French translation course, Français 322, because I have the conviction that it would give students the opportunity to read a text written in an interlanguage. Beside, translating *Je parle camerounais* gives foreign language student as opportunity to engage with a text that is hybridized. In one of our online discussion forums, a student wondered aloud: "Given the differences discussed between Camfranglais and hexagonal French, I wonder how it might be possible to accurately convey the author's intent regarding those differences. In her text, Fouda makes a point of highlighting linguistic and cultural differences between Cameroon and France... When the purpose of a text is to celebrate linguistic differences, can a translation alone be enough to get the point across, or would it be necessary to provide the reader with an aside explaining the significance of the impact of culture on language?"(ACE, February 9, 2014). This is a loaded question that remains unexplored to date. This is certainly a gray area that calls for research.

Reading *Je parle camerounais: pour un renouveau francofaune* has enabled my students to come to terms with the fact that there are as many variants of French as there are varieties of English in the world today. French is heterogeneous—there is *Camfranglais* in Cameroon, *Nouchi* in Côte d'Ivoire, *Franglais* in Canada, *creole-based* French in Francophone Caribbean and *Bislama* in the Francophone island of Vanuatu. This brings us to, perhaps, the most important question in this chapter: how is a text like Fouda's novel to be taught? In grabbling with this question, I have deemed it expedient to adopt an exegetic socio-cultural pedagogical model for teaching *Je parle camerounais: pour un renouveau francofaune*. The rationale for this choice is that Fouda's novel is an ethnographic text with a cultural substratum that calls for elucidation, such as has been illustrated in the examples above. The instructor has to interpret the situational dimensions that account for the holistic meaning of the text. Without a proper understanding of the non-textual components of the text, any attempt at teaching it would be a non-starter.

Arguing along similar lines, House (977) points out that the "semantico-stylistic interpretation of a literary text should be considered the most important aspect of exegesis in the translation process...we have to deal with details which are often hardly perceivable, yet are nonetheless significant since they inform us about the artistic type not by means of themes, composition and transformation of reality, but by delicate stylistic nuances" (68). Anyone teaching *Je parle camerounais* has to grapple with the latent significations embedded in the author's diction, turns of phrase and neologisms in order to be able to convey themes and author's intent to students unfamiliar with the socio-cultural matrix from which the novel sprouted. Fouda's text is not the only stylistically challenging novel written in Francophone Cameroon. Fonkou's *Moi taximan* (2001) harbors similar hurdles as the critical analysis in Chapter Six reveals.

Chapter 5

Fictionalizing Camfranglais in Fonkou's *Moi taximan*

Gabriel Kuitche Fonkou's *Moi taximan* seems to defy comprehension on account of the Africanized nature of the French language in which the novel is crafted as the following sentence shows: "Dans l'après midi, je devais rembourser de l'argent dans une tontine des ressortissants de mon village natal" (7) [In the afternoon, I had to pay back money I had borrowed from members of a *tontine* of people from my village.] The word 'tontine' is a neologism that describes a 'thrift society' where members contribute and borrow money when the need arises.[29] Lexical truncation is another word formative process used adeptly by Fonkou for the purpose of adding local color and flavor to his narrative: "J'avais remarqué dès les premiers jours que certains collègues clandos ne s'arrêtaient pas aux barrières de contrôle, ou que quand ils s'y arrêtaient, c'était pour échanger avec les contrôleurs des plaisanteries puis repartir sans avoir servi ni le café ni la bière" (12) [I had noticed from the onset that some clando colleagues never stopped at the police checkpoint, or only stopped to crack jokes with the controllers and leave without serving coffee or beer]. Fonkou's recourse to the word 'clando' could pose comprehension problems. Kouega

---

[29] An annuity, or loan, based on a group of annuities that are shared among several people with the provision that as each person dies his share is spread among those remaining, and the entire amount accrues to the survivor of them all. This term also refers to the members of the group collectively.

(2013) defines 'clando' as "a private car illegally used as a taxi"(164) as this excerpt shows: "Pour siba chez lui, tu take d'abord le clando, puis le bendskin à l'entrée "[To go to his place, you take first a taxi and then a motorcycle at the entrance](164).The word 'clando' also refers to a taxi driven by a driver who does not possess the legal documentation that gives him the right to drive a taxi. Sometimes, Cameroonians use the word 'clando' to describe a private car used to transport passengers illegally. 'Clando' derives from the word 'clandestine'.

Like Fouda, Fonkou resorts to the technique of compounding in an attempt to acquaint his readers with the thought patterns of Camfranglais speakers: "Les premiers contacts avec les mange-mille et les gendarmes coûtent cher, mais par la suite, tout le monde se connaît et il s'établit comme un contrat tacite"(12). [The first encounters with the mange-mille and gendarmes often cost much, but with time, people get to know one another and a sort of tacit contract is established.] 'Mange-mille' is a Camfranglais derogatory term used in Cameroon to talk about corrupt police officers who take bribes. It should be noted that the French used by Fonkou in this novel has been described as "le français langue africaine" by Mendo Zé (1999).Certain camfranglais neologisms are hard to decipher unless the reader is familiar with the lexicon of this language. As Nstobe et al would have it, "Il faut absolument connaître la signification de ces mots dans leurs contextes spécifiques" (90) [You really have to know the meanings and contextual usage of these words.] The difficulty stems from the fact that camfranglophones frequently borrow from indigenous languages to embellish their parlance as this proverbial expression shows: " L'enfant qui vit près de la chefferie ne craint pas le 'mekwum'" (14).

[The child who lives near the palace does not fear the 'mekwum'] The word 'mekwum' is an indigenous language word that refers to a masked dancer belonging in a village secret society.[30] The following excerpt is rich in borrowings from vernacular languages spoken in Cameroon: "Dès que je me trouvais au milieu de cette foule ce furent d'interminables poignées de mains d'une vigueur à vous déséquilibrer, d'interminable 'nge pin', 'a pon', 'a bha'a, toutes les expressions de l'approbation et de la satisfaction"(93)[As soon as I found myself in this crowd, we shook hands incessantly and so vigorously that one could lose one's equilibrium, endless 'nge pin', 'a pon', 'a bha'a, expressions of approbation and satisfaction.]

Oftentimes, camfranglophones embellish their discourse with ideophones in an attempt to translate the spoken word into writing: "C'est pratiquement toutes les personnes présentes qui s'écriaient 'Oueuh! Oueuh! Oueuh!'"(98) [Literally, everyone present shouted 'Oueuh! Oueuh! Oueuh!']The expression 'oueuh' also spelled 'weh-heh' is an interjection of compassion or pity. The reality of contemporary Cameroonian literature is that within it, oral traditions coexist with the encroaching print tradition. The translation process that takes place in Cameroonian prose fiction involves the transition from orality to the written word. It is perhaps for this specific reason that Emmanuel Obiechina argues:

> We are aware that writers are drawing elaborately from West African folklore, traditional symbols and images, and traditional turns of speech, to invest their writing with a truly West African sensibility and flavor"(143)

---

[30]Esoteric and occultist group

Arguing along similar lines, Scheub concludes his "A Review" (1985) with an emphatic statement in support of the view that there is an orality/literacy continuum in contemporary African literature:

> There is an unbroken continuity in African verbal art forms, from interacting oral genres to such literary productions as the novel and poetry...The early literary traditions were beneficiaries of the oral genres, and there is no doubt that the epic and its hero are predecessors of the novel and its central characters" (1)

Scheub's argument in support of the claim that the oral narrative is the antecedent of the contemporary African novel is cogent as our analysis of *Moi taximan* illustrates. *Moi taximan* is replete with French words that have undergone semantic metamorphosis as this statement indicates: "Je tombai sur Massa Yo alors que je venais d'essuyer deux semaines de chômage" (28) [I ran into Massa Yo after having spent two weeks without a job.] 'Massa' is a deformation of the English word 'Master.' This word has another meaning according to the definition provided by Kouega: "an address term meaning 'my friend'" (234). He uses an example to drive home the point: "Massa, comment tu go? [My friend, how are you today? Thus, 'massa' is synonymous with other terms of phatic communion provided by Kouega such as "tara" (295), "capo"(156), "gars"(196), "combi"(166), and "pote"(267).The dissident attitude of camfranglais speakers has caused some linguistic theorists to describe the advent of this nascent Cameroonian language as a transgression of the grammatical canons of the French language. As discussed above, Ntsobé et al perceive camfranglais as linguistic invasion. To put this differently, the quintessence of Camfranglais is the deconstruction of the grammatical conventions of the French language. As Kourouma would have it, Fonkou takes the liberty of toying with *une langue classique trop rigide pour que sa pensée s'y meuve.*

A sizeable number of Camfranglais words used in *Moi taximan* are related to the taxi industry as seen in the excerpt below: "Vous n'aviez qu'à tchouquer..." (29) [You only had to kick start it]. The word 'tchouquer,' also spelled 'chuker' translates the act of kick starting a car, generally when the battering is flat or the ignition system is defective. It also has sexual innuendoes: "to have sex"(Kouega, 163). Young Cameroonians tend to use 'tchouquer' or 'chuquer' to describe sexual intercourse, especially when they find themselves among adults. The trope of litotes[31] enables them to veil the impact of crude words on the sensibility of the prudish.

The rationale of this sort of linguistic manipulation is to conceal the meaning of certain taboo words from adults for the sake of propriety. These examples go a long way to buttress the contention that Fonkou's novel is not only a linguistic hybrid but is also a sociological novel.[32] The novelist has succeeded in writing an ethnographic novel[33] in the

---

[31]Litotes is a figure of speech in which understatement is employed for rhetorical effect, principally via double negatives. For example, rather than saying that something is attractive (or even very attractive), one might merely say it is "not unattractive. "Litotes is a form of understatement, always deliberate and with the intention of emphasis.

[32]A sociological novel is defined as a work of fiction that focuses on the sociological and economic conditions of characters or events. These sorts of novels are also known as social problem novels.

[33]An ethnographic novel is a work of fiction based on cultural mores.

French language by having recourse to the literary technique of indigenization.

Indigenization of the French language is evident in the following sentence: "Justine était généralement vêtue d'un 'kabba' par-dessus duquel elle avait noué un pagne" (130) [Justine was always dressed in a 'kabba' over which she tied a loincloth.] 'Kabba' is a loanword from Duala, one of the vernacular languages spoken in Cameroon. Kouega (2013) defines the term as "a type of gown worn by pregnant women" (213) and provides this example to buttress his point: "How tu put les kaba tous les jours et tu ne put plus les jeans, no? Tu hide quelque chose? Tu as tcha? " [How come you put on gowns everyday and not jeans anymore? Are you hiding something? Are you pregnant?](213) These examples bear testimony to the fact that *Moi taximan* is a novel in which native tongue words and expressions jostle for space with standard French lexical items and turns of phrase. The technique of 'coinage' enables Fonkou to achieve this objective.

Coinage enables the novelist to find words that appropriately convey the mindset and worldview of his characters as seen in this statement: "Entre deux clients, Justine et sa mère participaient activement à l'entretien de la chaude ambiance du secteur des 'bayam sellam': potins, querelles simulées, plaisanteries et fausses confidences bruyantes y provoquaient de gros éclats de rire" (131)[Between two customers, Justine and her mother took part in the heated discussions that animated the 'bayam sellam' section of the market: gossip, fake quarrels, jokes and noisy false pretences that caused outbursts of laughter.] As explained in a previous chapter, 'bayam sellam', is a compound word derived from Cameroonian Pidgin English.

It is used in this novel to describe industrious market women whom the protagonist describes as "des revendeuses, cette catégorie de commerçantes aggressives sans les lesquelles nos marchés perdraient leur âme"(130) [Retail traders, this category of aggressive market women without whom our markets would lose their liveliness.] 'Bayam sellam' trade consists precisely of buying and selling foodstuff bought wholesale at the lowest possible prices in the rural areas (farms and plantations in the villages) to resell by retail in urban areas in Cameroon (Bafoussam, Douala, Nkongsamba, Yaoundé, etc.)

The title of Fonkou's novel—*Moi taximan*—calls for a comment. The first half of the title "Moi" is a tonic pronoun. Tonic pronouns are used for the purpose of emphasis. Thus, when Fonkou's narrator says "Moi," he attempts to draw attention onto himself, an invitation extended to the reader to listen to his story attentively. The second part of the title is a compound noun derived from two words—"taxi" and "man." 'Taximan' is a hybrid word coined by camanglophones in reference to a cab driver. Kouega(2013)defines the term as "a taxi driver"(296) and refers readers to the following example: " J'ai gi mon dernier kolo au taximan et il a forget de me rembourser" [I gave my last one thousand Franc note to a taxi driver and he forgot to give me the change](296). Notice that the word 'kolo' used in this excerpt is a reference to Cameroonian currency, the CFA franc[34]. Kouega (2013) defines 'kolo' as "one thousand CFA

---

[34]CFA stood for *Colonies françaises d'Afrique* ("French colonies of Africa). The CFA franc was created on 26 December 1945. The CFA franc (in French: *franc CFA*, or colloquially *franc*) is the name of two currencies used in Africa which are guaranteed by the French treasury. The two CFA franc currencies are the West African CFA franc and the Central African CFA franc. Although theoretically separate, the two CFA

francs" (217). Here is the example he gives using the word 'kolo': "J'ai buy *ça* kolo" [I bought it for one thousand francs] (217). He further observes that 'kolo-fap' refers to one thousand five hundred francs as in "Il gagne kolo-fap la journée" [He earns one thousand five hundred francs a day, that is around one pound fifty] (217).

The slang spoken by Fonkou's characters is an interlanguage fabricated by youths "désireux de s'exprimer entre eux de telle sorte qu'ils ne soient compréhensibles que par les locuteurs…capables de décoder les termes empruntés à l'anglais, au pidgin English ou aux langues camerounaises"(Ntsobé et al, 2008, p. 9) [Interested in conversing with one another in such a manner that what they say is only intelligible to initiates…capable of decoding the meanings of terms culled from English, Pidgin and indigenous Cameroonian languages.] Put differently, some lexical items employed by this novelist are loans from Cameroonian Creole (pidgin English) as this example shows: "Au bout de la journée le plus souvent chacun de nous affichait un sourire de contentement et nous nous quittions à la nuit tombante sur de vigoureuses poignées de mains prolongées par un 'toss'…"(13). [More often than not, at the end of the day, each one of us wore a smile of satisfaction; we parted at nightfall after vigorously shaking hands and saying 'toss.'] Fonkou's protagonist describes the word "toss" as "salut du bout des pouces et des majeurs entrecroisés puis séparés dans un vif frottement sonore" (13) [Form of

---

franc currencies are effectively interchangeable. The reason for their creation was the weakness of the French franc immediately after World War II. When France ratified the Bretton Woods Agreement in December 1945, the French franc was devalued in order to set a fixed exchange rate with the US dollar. New currencies were created in the French colonies to spare them the strong devaluation, thereby facilitating exports to France.

handshake with the tips of the thumb and middle-fingers intertwined, followed by a quick separation and loud sound.]

Pidgin has enriched Camfranglais enormously as seen in the following statement: "La journée d'hier a été djidja."(19) [Yesterday was djidja.] 'Djidja,' a loanword from Pidgin English, derives from the English word "ginger." A spelling variant of this word is word *ndjinja*. Echu (1991) notes that the word *ndjinja (*spelling variant) means 'ginger' in Cameroon Popular English (CPE) but signifies 'difficult' when used in Camfranglais parlance. Whereas the word is used in CPE as a noun, it becomes an adjective in Camfranglais. Usages like this bears testimony to the linguistic creativity of Camfranglais speakers.

Kouega (2013) defines the term "djidja" as it "hard, something difficult to do; a nut hard to crack" (197) as in the following example: "Le test du prof était djidja" [The test of the professor was ginger] (197). In other words, the test given by the professor was difficult. In standard French, the equivalent of this expression would be "une mer à boire" [an uphill task].

Oftentimes, Fonkou's characters resort to the technique of clipping as a word formative process: "En même temps, ses bras se livraient à des gestes qu'il voulait impérieux, pour m'intimer de m'arrêter illico" (21) [At the same time, he made majestic arm gestures as if to stop me right away.] The word 'illico' is a deformation of 'illegal,' used in this context to convey the notion of imprudent attitude. Kouega (2013) observes that the technique of shortening "subsumes back formation, initialism and clipping" (59). He further observes that clipping is a process which consists in removing parts of a word. As he puts it, "The clipped elements may be at the initial position(fore clipping, front clipping or aphesis…), medial position(mid clipping or final position(hind clipping, back clipping or apocope....)" (60)

Fonkou seems to have a predilection for hind clipping. He frequently suppresses the terminal syllables of words as seen in the following excerpt: "Je n'en sais rien, espèce de Bami."(24) [I have no idea, you Bami fellow.] The word 'Bami' is an abbreviation of 'Bamileke,' one of the ethnic groups in Cameroon loathed by other Cameroonians for their ruthless money-mongering and resourcefulness. Used the way Fonkou does here, the word conveys derogatory undertones.

As these examples illustrate, clipping is a favourite word formation technique constantly exploited by Camfranglais speakers to create new words that portray the prism through which they perceive social reality. It is tempting to draw the conclusion that Fonkou's novel is in the main a re-capturing in print of the oral discourses of Cameroonians—a palimpsest of sorts or an imitation[35] of that which already existed. However, to do so would be tantamount to discounting the literary capital he has made out of linguistic experimentation. Fonkou makes abundant use of the technique of linguistic innovation to portray both the socio-cultural realities of Cameroon and the significant influence of pidgin on Cameroonian French. Arguing along the same lines, Echu (2006) posits that "Popular French and Camfranglais are two pidginized varieties of French that have developed in Cameroon, the first out of the necessity to

---

[35] A palimpsest is a manuscript from a scroll or book from which the text has been scraped or washed off so that it can be used again. It literally means "scraped clean and used again."The term has come to be used in a similar context in a variety of disciplines, notably architectural archaeology and geomorphology. For more on this subject matter, read Gerald Genette's *Palimpsests: Literature in the Second Degree on*(1997) *or its French translation, Palimpsestes: la littérature au second degree*(1982).

communicate among people from heterogeneous backgrounds and the second as a secret code among young people"(2). He further observes that although both Cameroonian Popular French and Camfranglais are basically oral varieties of Standard French employed for informal interaction, they are sometimes written. Such is the case when used by humorists to create humor.

Fonkou mixes languages[36] purposefully in a bid to underscore the polyglossic context from which his text sprouted as this example illustrates: "Et maintenant, vous êtes gonflés à bloc pour le comeback que vous voulez effectuer"(180) [Now, you are inflated enough for the comeback that you are set to accomplish.] By inserting the English word 'comeback' in a French language text the novelist seems to suggest that readers of his novel are expected to be not just bicultural but bilingual as well. The need to possess both translingual and transcultural competences in order to successfully decipher the latent significations embedded in Fonkou's text is made all the more evident through the use of culture-specific expressions to portray indigenous mores as seen in this example: "La plus grosse surprise se situa le dimanche où la réunion des femmes

---

[36]Code-mixing refers to the mixing of two or more languages or language varieties in speech. Some scholars use the terms "code-mixing" and "code-switching" interchangeably, especially in studies of syntax, morphology, and other formal aspects of language. While linguists who are primarily interested in the structure or form of code-mixing may have relatively little interest to separate code-mixing from code-switching, some sociolinguists have gone to great lengths to differentiate the two phenomena. For these scholars, code-switching is associated with particular pragmatic effects, discourse functions, or associations with group identity. In this tradition, the terms code-mixing or language alternation are used to describe more stable situations in which multiple languages are used without such pragmatic effects.

de mon village vint laver l'enfant"(186) [The biggest surprise came on a Sunday, the day when the association of women from my village came to wash the baby.] 'Laver l'enfant' is a local expression that describes the cultural ritual during which the birth of a baby is celebrated by family members. In Fonkou's native tongue, this ritual is called "le yaal, à la fois danse et chants pour célébrer la naissance de l'enfant" (187) [the yaal, both song and dance to celebrate the birth of a child.]

In a nutshell, it goes without saying that if up to a certain point, each postcolonial writer has to re-invent language, the situation of Cameroonian writers residing out of France is peculiar in that for them, French is not an acquisition; rather it is an occasion for constant mutations and modifications. Engaged as they are, in the game of language, these writers have to create their own language of fiction, in a multilingual context often affected by signs of diglossia. Contemporary Cameroonian Francophone literature exists at the interface of French as a hegemonic language and its indigenized variant. Incontrovertible evidence of otherness in this new form of literature is recourse to modes of writing distinctive by linguistic variance. In his text *The Francophone African Text: Translation and the Postcolonial Experience* (2006), Gyasi argues along similar lines when he observes that African Francophone fiction writers create "a French that is in consonance with the new African environment and the characters that live in it...."(77). He describes this linguistic demand on the writer's part as an act of defiance. As the foregoing analysis suggests, Fonkou's *Moi taximan* qualifies to be categorized as a hybrid text engendered by a plurality of 'voices', and the multilingual context of its creation. Fonkou has written a multi-layered text that demands of readers to be both multilingual and multicultural in order to unravel the underlying textual significations, the more so because *Moi taximan* functions as a site of cultural appropriation and linguistic resistance. This holds true for the works of another Cameroonian novelist, Patrice Nganang, whose novel we shall analyse in the next chapter.

Chapter 6

Streetwise French in Nganang's *Temps de chien*

With the publication of *Temps de chien*(2001) Nganang emerged as a writer noted for his creative use of the French language. Any discussion on this novel that glosses over the function of language would amount to parochial textual analysis. One can hardly speak of Nganang's narrative technique without reckoning with the linguistic novelty that characterizes his style of writing. *Temps de chien* addresses the language question in Cameroonian literature. Nganang focuses on the manner in which the African writer employs language to wed form to content. *Temps de chien* is a masterpiece written partially in Camfranglais, otherwise known as streetwise French. It has been translated into English as *Dog Days* (2006). By adapting a narrative style that borders on linguistic subversion Nganang establishes a mode of writing that is analogous to Ahmadou Kourouma's *malinkelization* of French in *Les soleils des indépendances* (1970). The manipulative devices that Nganang uses play the significant role of reproducing the source language culture through the process of metonymic embodiment. As Wendt observes, "Evidently, many writers believe that by such means they are keeping faith with their culture and transporting it into the new medium" (28).

Code-switching enables Nganang to make French bear the weight of his African worldview. Reading the novel gives one the impression that Nganang is determined to tweak the language of Voltaire out of shape. He subverts the French language for three main reasons. Firstly, he intends to debunk the myth according to which Africans do not have languages comparable to the languages of white folks. Secondly, he has the desire to underscore the fact that writing African literature in European languages leaves much to be desired on account of cultural gaps. Thirdly, Nganang wants to drive home the point that Africans cannot and should not write like their ex-colonial masters considering the fact that Africans are offshoots of linguistic and cultural miscegenation.

Nganang attempts to appropriate French by bringing it under the influence of Cameroonian indigenous languages, Camfranglais and Pidgin English. He interpolates vernacular lexes into the French language as seen in the following example: "Menmà, si j'avais encore ta force, j'aurai fait autre chose que de m'asseoir derrière mon comptoir et regarder passer la vie!" (*Temps de chien* 148) [Menma, if I still had your strength, I'd have done something other than sit behind my counter and watch life go by! (*Dog Days* 101-2)] The word "Menma" is an Africanism[37] borrowed from the Medùmba language[38] spoken in Cameroon. It could be translated as "brother or sister," with a dose of affection. By having recourse to this vernacular word, Nganang is able to convey the notion of filial relationship and love to his readers

---

[37]Africanisms are words or practices that came from Africa to North America. Africanisms refer to characteristics of African culture and people that can be traced through societal practices and institutions of the African diaspora.

[38]Medumba is a Grassfields language of Cameroon. The people who speak it originate from the Nde division with the main settlements in Bangangte, Bakong, Bangoulap, Bahouoc, Bagnoun and Tonga of the West region in Cameroon. It is one major Bamileke language. Educational materials, literature, and dictionaries for the language are produced by the Comité de Langue pour l'Etude et la Production des Œuvres Bamiléké-Medumba (CEPOM), based in Bangangte.

through the prism of his native culture. He personifies the word "life" in his text by endowing it with the quality of mobility in order to emphasize the African belief in man's dependence on the cosmos. Nganang's attempt at indigenizing the French language is evident in his imitation of local speech patterns as seen in the following example:

> Regardez-moi un énergumène comme ça qui vient dans un bar comme celui-ci où les gens me respectent dire que c'est lui qui me gère, *anti zambaouam*! Il ose même dire qu'il voulait m'épouser. Regardez donc le mari de Mini Minor. Dites-moi vraiment, vous qui me connaissez: est-ce que je mérite un têtard comme ça …? Vraaaiiiment, même les cauchemars ont des limites. Moi la femme de ce cancrelat-ci! (66)
> [But the rest of you, just look at this raving lunatic, who comes into a bar like this where people respect me and says that he is keeping me, *anti zamba ouam!* He even dares to say he wants to marry me. Take a look at Mini Minor's husband. Now tell me, you all who know me: do I deserve a polliwog like that? …. Reeeeally, even nightmares have limits! Me the wife of this cockroach!] (*Dog* Days, 44)

The passage above contains an Africanism purposefully inserted into the discourse in a bid to endow the novel with a cultural substratum. The interjection *anti zamba ouam* is culled from the Beti language. It could be translated as "my gosh!) Kouega (2013) defines the term as follows: "an injection meaning 'Gosh!'(321) He maintains that the expression is often used by youngsters from the Beti area of Cameroon. Throughout the narrative the reader enjoys not only the writer's verve at storytelling but also his adroitness at linguistic engineering. Notice that linguistic manipulation is evident of Nganang's use of the standard French word "gérer" in the passage above. *Gérer* in metropolitan French could be defined as 'to manage' or 'to direct' the affaires of a company or business enterprise. However, in Camfranglais "gérer" takes on the secondary meaning of 'to own a concubine." By desemanticing the standard word *gérer*, Nganang succeeds in Africanizing French. He resorts to code-switching as a technique for transposing Cameroonian sociocultural realities and linguistic specificities into the French language in *Temps de chien*.

Code-switching as a Narrative Technique in Nganang's *Temps de chien*

The particularity of his style resides in the presence of bits and pieces (if not chunks) of Cameroonian languages in the text. In his attempt to transpose the speech mannerisms of Cameroonians into French, the novelist employs a variety of linguistic codes, a phenomenon which Haugan refers to as "the alternate use of two languages, including everything from the introduction of a single unassimilated word up to a complete sentence or more into the context of another language" (Quoted in Omole, 58). *Temps de chien* harbors an amalgam of codes—French, English, Cameroonian Pidgin, Camfranglais and numerous indigenous languages. It is a novel in which street-talk, also known as "Kam-Tok," "Camspeak" or "Majunga Talk" (Ze Amvela, 56) blends freely with conventional French to produce a new code whose effect on the reader is exhilarating.

In an interview he granted Taina Tervonen, Nganang had this to say about the stylistic choices he had to make in writing this novel: "La rue a une avance singulière tant sur les journalistes que sur les écrivains. Ce roman essaie de se mettre à l'école de la rue.... L'imagination et l'oralité des rues a fabriqué ces personages qui existent et que j'ai mis dans mon roman" (105) [The street exerts a unique pull both on journalists and writers. This novel attempts to depict the street school....The imagination and orality of the street have produced the characters that exist and have been inserted into my novel.] Speaking in a similar vein, Bengoéchea (2007) observes: "L'écriture de Patrice Nganang peut paraître atypipque dans la mesure où elle s'inscrit dans une réalité tant sociale que linguistique;c'est-à-dire que ses romans sont l'objet d'un ancrage sociolinguistique particulier marqué par le plurilinguisme et le contact entre la français et le substrat linguistique camerounais"(9)[The writing of Patrice Nganang could appear to be atypical in the sense that it is anchored in both social and linguistic matrices; in other words, his novels are the object of a given sociolinguistic anchorage characterized by plurilingualism and contact between French and languages in the Cameroonian substratum.]

The focus of this chapter is code-switching, a device employed expertly by Nganang in his narrative. In his attempt to translate the speech patterns of indigenous populations into written French, the novelist switches codes constantly. Code-switching enables him to transpose native languages, Pidgin English and Camfranglais into Standard French language.

Camfranglais

Nganang resorts to camfranglais expressions frequently for self-expression and local color as seen in the following excerpt: "Ma woman no fit chasser me for ma long dis-donc!

Après tout, ma long na ma long!"(80)[My woman no fit chasser me for ma long, dis donc! Après tout, ma long na ma long!](*Dog Days*, 54) The translator resorted to *calque* as a translation device in the passage above. Jones(1997) defines the term 'calque' as "a copy of an original. It is a translated borrowing: the borrowing of a foreign word or group of words by the literal translation of its components" (53). The translator did a laudable job of providing a footnote in the glossary to shed light on the meaning of the urban slang as follows: "My woman can't throw me out of my house, I tell you! After all, my house is my house!"(208) The word "long" changes grammatical category from adjective to noun. This translation technique is called 'transposition.' Jones defines *transposition* as "a translation device which involves a change between grammatical categories, notably nouns, verbs, adjectives, adverbs and prepositions, from the S.L. to the T.L" (77). In Nganang's novel, *long* refers to the speaker's "home."

The translator uses the same technique to translate the following passage: "La voix d'un lycéen lui disait: comme d'habitude, Mama Mado. Et ma maîtresse connaissait son goût. La voix d'un autre exigeait, put oya soté, for jazz must do sous-marin." (84)[A student's voice would say: the usual, Mama Mado, and my mistress knew just what he wanted. Another's voice would order, put oya soté, for jazz must do sous-marin.](*Dog Days*, 57) The term "oya" is a Pidgin English word for "oil," in this case oil used in cooking. "Jazz" is a slang word for 'beans.' Kouega (2013) defines *jazz* as "cooked beans usually eaten with 'beignets' at the 'beignetariat'" (210). The expression "jazz sous-marin" could be translated as "beans submerged in oil." Cameroonians use the term 'jazz' to describe the trumpet-like sound that one's stomach would make if one ate badly cooked beans. Americans call beans "noisy food." The sentence above could be translated into English as: "A student's voice would say: as usual, Mama Mado, and my mistress knew just what he wanted. Another's voice would order: put enough oil so that the jazz look like submarines."

At times, Nganang employs Camfranglais expressions in conjunction with Pidgin English expressions for the purpose of creating the burlesque[39] as seen in the following example: "Le silence des mille regards du quartier la suivait. Une véritable small no be sick." (67) [The silence of the neighbourhood's thousand staring eyes followed her. A real small no be sick.] (*Dog Days,* 45) The expression 'small no be sick,', also written 'simol no be sick' in Francophone Cameroonian Pidgin derives from the medical lexicon. Kouega (2013) defines the term as "a popular Chinese balm called 'Temple of Heaven' and used for the treatment of minor ailments like bruises, wounds, etc." (287). It refers to a balm considered by most Cameroonians to be a panacea for all kinds of ailments on account of its supposed efficacy. Its use in reference to a woman, Mini Minor, owner of the "Chantiers de la République" tavern, is figurative and could be translated as: 'Don't mess with her; she may look small but she's is very dangerous or powerful.' Nganang makes abundant use of code-switching in an attempt to translate Cameroonian turns of phrase, worldview and imagination into the French language.

The technique of code-switching enables him to blend several disparate codes together to form a third code, a canon

---

[39]Burlesque is a literary, dramatic or musical work intended to cause laughter by caricaturing the manner or spirit of serious works, or by ludicrous treatment of their subjects.

that may render the novel rather hard to decipher as noted by Aurelie Lefebvre (2007):

> *Temps de chien* présente une écriture qui se veut différentielle dans la mesure où elle ne correspond pas toujours à la norme du français standard... Les énonces dus aux narrateurs sont écrits dans un style plutôt classique, mais pas toujours. Le français y est émaillé de particularités lexicales (emprunts, néologismes, calques, etc.) et fait parfois appel à différents registres du soustenu au populaire), si bien que l'écriture s'avère souvent singulière(40).
>
> [*Temps de chien* is a text intended to express otherness in the sense that it is not written in standard French.... Utterances attributed to characters are written in a style that is more or less classical but not always. The French language is tainted with lexical particularisms (borrowing, neologism, calques, etc.) that sometimes call for recourse to different registers sustained by popular usage that often renders the writing peculiar.]

Nganang uses Camfranglais for the purpose of underscoring the socio-linguistic backdrop against which *Temps de chien* is written as this example shows:

> "If he no fit tchop he moni, n'est-ce pas la mbok-là va l'aider?"(253)[If he couldn't spend his money fast enough that mbok was going to help him, isn't that right?"] (*Dog Days,* 176)

The term "tchop" is used in Francophone Cameroonian Pidgin English as the equivalent of "spend" and "eat." In

Anglophone Cameroonian Pidgin, it is written "chop." "Moni" comes from "money," and "mbok" is a slang word for "whore." It is also spelled 'bok' (Kouega, 2013). The word "he" could be translated as "his." The entire sentence would be appropriately rendered as: "If he didn't know how to spend his money, this whore would help him spend it, isn't that right?" By switching codes, Nganang draws the reader's attention to the plurilingual matrix from which his work takes root. He infuses his writing with a plethora of languages spoken in Cameroon to represent the vitality of oral discourse that one would hear in the streets of Yaounde and its neighbourhoods. More often than not, characters in the novel resort to Pidgin in a bid to communicate effectively with people that share this linguistic code.

Recourse to Pidgin English

Temps de chien is replete with expressions culled from Pidgin English[40] as the following example illustrates: "Et mon

---

[40]Cameroonian Pidgin English is an English-based Creole. About 5% of Cameroonians are native speakers of the language, while an estimated 50% of the population speaks it in some form. Pidgin English has been in active use in Cameroon for over 500 years. It started in the Slave Trade years, resisted a German ban during the German annexation period (1884-1914) and survived post-independence neglect. It took flight when it became a makeshift language used in the plantations. Today, it has left the plantations for the homes and other domains of public life. The first attempt to codify this language was made by the Catholic Church, which used it to produce a number of religious materials including the catechism. Five varieties are currently recognized: Grafi Kamtok, the variety used in the grassfields and often referred to as 'Grafi Talk', liturgical Kamtok— this variety has been used by the Catholic Church for three quarters of a century. Francophone Kamtok is now used mainly in towns such as Douala, Bafoussam and Yaoundé and by Francophones talking to Anglophones who do not speak French. Limbe Kamtok is spoken mainly in the southwest coastal area around the port that used to

maître lui, se retranchant dans son pidgin de crise, tout en déchirant sur son visage un bleu: Dan sapak i day kan-kan-o." (52)[As for my master, he'd fall back into pidgin, his dialect of disaster, cursing the whores as he tore his face into a sick smile: 'Dan sapak i day for kan-kan-o.](*Dog Days*, 35) The code-switching in this excerpt is an indication that Massa Yo is straddling both the English and French linguistic spheres. Nganang spices his text with Pidgin English expressions to make his language respond realistically to the mentality of his characters. "Sapak" is slang for "whore." This holds true for the expression "kan-kan," a Pidgin English expression for "kind" (variety). "Day" (often written "de" or "deh") is a Pidgin word derived from the English word "there." The word "dan" is the pidginized form of the demonstrative adjective "that" In *Temps de chien*, recourse to Pidgin English is not to be perceived as an indication of the character's low level of education or inability to communicate effectively in standard French. Oftentimes, Nganang's characters communicate in Pidgin English as a sign of informality for phatic communion. The sentence above could be translated as "There are all kinds of whores in this vicinity." The expression "kan kan-o" expresses "variety." Echu(2006) notes that the "pidginization processes operational in the two varieties clearly illustrate the relationship between language contact and cultural dynamism, the two speech forms being an expression of the culture of the highly multicultural Cameroonian setting"(1).

---

be called Victoria and is now Limbe. Bororo Kamtok is the variety that is spoken by Bororo cattle traders, many of whom travel through Nigeria and Cameroon. For more on Cameroon Pidgin English, see Mbassi-Manga (1976).

Some Pidginized expressions in *Temps de chien* harbor sexual innuendos. For example, the following comment made by Massa Yo about Mini Minor is bawdy: " Quand elle avait disparu au loin, mon maître disait rêveur: Dan tendaison for dan woman na big big hein?"(69)[When she has disappeared in the distance, my master would say, still dreaming of her ample behind: Dan tendaison for dan woman na big big huh?] (*Dog Days*, 47). The reduplication of the word "big" translates the notion of "extremity." Echu posits that "Camfranglais utterances are strongly marked by reduplication, which is the repetition of morphological and lexical elements within an utterance"(8).He further notes that such repetitions emphasize the intensity or duration of an action, express argumentative and diminutive values, or simply constitute an inherent feature of one of the indigenous contact languages. He provides the following examples to underscore the importance of reduplication in Camfranglais: *doucement doucement* (very slowly or very gently), *nayor nayor* (very slowly or very gently), *penya penya* (very new or in very good state), *beaucoup beaucoup* (in great quantity), *un peu un peu* (very little or in very small quantity), *depuis depuis* (a very long time ago), *nyama nyama* (very small; of little significance or value), *keleng keleng* (a local type of spinach), *zouazoua* (illicit fuel sold clandestinely in Cameroon and believed to be smuggled from Nigeria) and *poto-poto* (mud or something of no value). "Tendaison" used in the excerpt above is the Pidgin word for "buttocks." In this passage, Mini Minor's buttocks are depicted as elephantine. The sentence could be translated as: "When she had disappeared in the distance, my master would say, still dreaming of her ample behind: That woman has extremely big buttocks, huh?"

Nganang's narrator resorts to the following Pidgin expression to describe the uncanny ways of robbers: "Femme, avait-il dit, tu n'as pas entendu ce qu'on raconte? Les voleurs ont déjà la potion pour se rendre invisibles ici dehors. N'est-ce pas hier ils sont entrés dans le salon de Massa Kokari et ont emporté sa télévision sous son nez? A di tell you" (50) [Woman, he said, haven't you heard what people are saying? Thieves already have a potion that makes them invisible out there. Don't you know that yesterday they went into Massa Kokari's living room and took his television right from under his nose? A di tell you] (*Dog Days*, 34). The emphatic "A di tell you" could be translated as: "Take it from me." Generally, Cameroonians employ an expression like this in a bid to dispel doubt especially when they sense disbelief on the part of the interlocutor. The word "Massa" is the pidgin equivalent of the English word "Mr." or "Master." These sociolects are appropriate in Nganang's text and speak to its linguistic plurality. Each linguistic variety invokes a specific type of discourse that is in synchrony with the social status of the interlocutor. *Temps de chien* is a hodgepodge of European and indigenous languages.

Indigenous languages

Nganang constantly borrows from the 248 vernacular languages spoken in Cameroon as seen in the following example culled from Fufuldé: "A ce moment une voix furieuse dit au dessous de moi: Kai wa laï!" (212) [At that moment I heard a furious voice above me: Kai wa laï!](148). Fufuldé is an indigenous language spoken in the northern regions of Cameroon "Kai wa laï!" is a swear expression which could be rendered as "Watch out!" It is an interjection expressing anger, reprisal or retaliation. It is interesting to note that speakers of Fulfulde borrowed this expression from speakers of Arabic. Fufuldé is not the only indigenous language from which Nganang borrows in order to domesticate the French language. He gleans words and expressions from the Beti language spoken in the Center Region of Cameroon as seen in this excerpt:

> "Quelques heures après leur arrestation, la voix de la Panthère traversa les chuchotements coupables de la cour du bar. "Mbe ke di? cria-t-il, mbe ils ont arrêté l'écrivain-a? Sè ? Nùm ke? Ntog a ya? Comment? Vous dites vrai? A tat'te!"(145)
> [A few hours after their arrest, Panther's voice cut through the guilty whispers of the bar courtyard. "Mbe ke di?" he screamed." They arrested the writer-a? Sè ? When? Why? Which way did they go? How? I don't believe it! A tat'te! It's a lie!"](*Dog Days*, 99).

Echu (2006) makes the following remarks about the influence of native tongues on the speech patterns of Cameroonians:

> Indigenous language calques are another main source of pidginization. Here, the interference of indigenous languages on CPF is at the morphosyntactic level. In short, while speaking French, certain speakers simply translate verbatim indigenous language expressions. This results in the introduction of apparently strange constructions in the French language, constructions that can only be understood and appreciated within the local context(14)

He provides the following examples to buttress his point: "Même les professeurs gâtent aussi les filles d'autrui."(14) (Even teachers have sexual relations with other people's daughters). In standard French this statement would be written as follows: "Même les professeurs entretiennent aussi des relations coupables avec les filles d'autrui." Indigenous language words used in *Temps de chien* without French language equivalents may be difficult to understand on account of cultural gaps. As Omole contends, "Even if a form of translation could be forged, it would inevitably mutilate the writer's meaning" (63). Some indigenized words in the text are anthroponyms—personal names, as seen in the following example : "On parlait de l'homme qui avait insulté tout le monde. Ce devrait être un nkoua, dit-on" (97) [People were talking about the man who had insulted everybody. He must be nkoua](*Dog Days,* 66). The word "nkoua" refers to people who hail from the Beti tribes in the Southern part of Cameroon. Another word that carries tribal undertones is "Bamiléké" (91, 96). "Medùmba" (91) is another anthroponym which Nganang defines in a footnote as "langue bantou du groupe bamiléké" (91).

Switching codes enables the novelist to fictionalize the belief systems of his characters. A classic example is the belief in Famla[41] as seen in this excerpt: "L'argent seul est ton ami, non? Je suis sûr qu'un jour on va seulement entendre que tu as vendu Soumi au famla ne ne ne" (147) [Money is your only friend, right? I'm sure that one day we're gonna hear you've sold Soumi to Famla] (*Dog Days,* 101). By alternating between French and an indigenous language, Medùmba, Nganang introduces an important element of acculturation into the narrative—the practice of witchcraft. By reverting to the

---

[41]Bamileke occult society notorious for its acts of sorcery

mother-tongue reduplication, "ne ne ne" the writer emphasizes the belief system peculiar to the Bamileke. The expression "ne ne ne" is used for the purpose of emphasis. It could be translated as "with no qualms." In other words, Massa Yo would "sell" his, son Soumi, to "Famla" with no pang of conscience. To "sell" someone to famla is to bewitch them. It should be noted that belief in the existence of Famla is a myth tenable only in cultish societies where people believe in death through witchcraft as the following sentence indicates: "A un Carrefour, une femme maudissait tous ceux qui venaient la nuit la manger. Elle faisait des gestes démentiels, et promettait de partir chez le père Soufo" 196) [At one intersection a woman was cursing those who came in the night to devour her. She was waving her hands around like crazy promising to go see Père Soufo, the miracle-working prophet of La Carrière](*Dog Days*, 136). In African cultures, the term "Père" sometimes shortened to "Pè" and translated as "Pa" in English is a form of address reserved for people of a certain age. It connotes respect for seniority. This is true for "Ma" derived from "Mère." Honorific titles play an essential role in African communities where it is taboo for youths to address parents and elders by first name. This is not unique to Africa. In Caribbean literature, onomastics plays an essential role as well. Chamoiseau underscores this cultural particularity when he uses the title "Pè" as a form of address for Soltène, an elderly character in his novel *Texaco* (1992).

The linguistic variety noticeable in *Temps de chien*—French, Pidgin English, Camfranglais, Beti, Medùmba, Fufuldé, Duala and a host of others—serve not only as socio-cultural signifiers but also as identity markers. The language of narration is principally French but the novelist switches codes when he deems it fit in order to translate the worldview, imagination and speech peculiarities of his people into written French. Nganang's constant recourse to puns (play on words) is noteworthy throughout the narrative. It could be inferred from these examples that signifying[42] is an essential component of Nganang's narrative style. He uses the technique of 'signifying' as a trope in which are subsumed several other rhetorical devices. *Temps de chien* is a hybrid text in which the characters look inward into Cameroonian cultures and outward to an imported French culture. Nganang's characters straddle this cultural divide by drawing from both the oral discourses of the streets and the European literate culture by which they have been deeply influenced.

As the aforementioned examples show, code-mixing is an effective cross-cultural communication device in *Temps de chien*. It enables the writer to transpose the cultural artefacts of Cameroonians into French as seen in the following passage: "Une fois mon maître demanda à Soumi de me donner une part du délicieux koki rouge et huileux qui gonflait son plat" (26) [Once my master asked Soumi to give me some of his delicious red and greasy koki that was piled up in his plate](*Dog Days,* 17).Kouega(2013) defines the term 'koki' as "a national meal of beans cake which was started up by the people of the coastal region of Cameroon" (217).The rendition of "koki rouge et huileux" as "red and greasy koki" is a free translation of sorts. Cameroonian Koki is not cooked in grease. It is cooked in red palm-oil. Koki is the name of a local dish indigenous to the Duala ethnic group in the Littoral

---

[42]In his work, *The Signifying Monkey: A theory of African-American Literary Criticism* (1989), Gates points out that 'signifying' "concerns itself with that which…we can represent as the playful puns on words that occupy the paradigmatic axis of language and which a speaker draws on for figurative substitutions."(48)

Region of Cameroon. It is made of ground beans mixed with numerous ingredients cooked in red palm-oil.

Nganang's text contains several extra-linguistic components which must be deciphered for a proper appreciation of his text as this excerpt indicates:

> Recroquevillé dorénavant dans son trou obscur de sa crise, mortifié par le souvenir de l'aisance dont il avait été abruptement sevré, émasculé par le bobolo sec aux arachides grillées qu'il devait maintenant manger le matin, à midi et le soir, mon maître ne tendait plus sa main vers moi pour me caresser le crâne(15)
> [Hunkered down from then on in the dark hole of his crisis, mortified by memories of the comfortable life from which he has been so abruptly weaned, emasculated by having to eat dry bobolo with grilled peanuts morning, noon and night, my master no longer reached out to caress my head](*Dog Days*, 10)

It should be noted that the expression 'matin, midi, soir'" could be rendered in English as all the time, all day long or permanently. 'Bobolo' is a dish made of ground cassava tuber wrapped in banana or plantain leaves. A cultural referent such as 'bobolo' may pose translation problems but some effort has to be made to render native tongue words accurately. Several indigenous terms transposed into *Temps de chien* have no French language equivalents. Examples include: 'koki' (26), 'bobolo' (15), 'maguida' (16), 'siscia' (112), 'ndoutou' and so forth. The term 'ndoutou' needs particular emphasis given that it poses a thorny translation problem as seen in the following passage: "Il frappa ses mains et dit: C'est du ndoutou, dis donc. Elle veut me gâter la journée" (205) [He clapped his hands and said: "It's just ndoutou, I tell you, bad luck. She wants to ruin my day"] (*Dog Days*, 142). Note that 'ndoutou' is worse than back luck. In Cameroonian discourse this word carries a deeper meaning than ill-luck. "Ndoutou" is a mishap that is likely to ruin one's entire day. This is because there is a myth among Cameroonians according to which a misfortune begets another. For instance, a beyam-sellam would tell her first customer to not bring her 'ndoutou' if the customer drove too hard a bargain. The reason is that these market women have the conviction that the first customer sets the pace for the day. Therefore, if things went wrong the first time it would recur throughout the day.

Indigenous language words and expressions have specific connotations in *Temps de chien* as this excerpt shows: "Des rumta, elles étaient, oui et lui Massa Yo saurait bien les tordre. Il saurait leur montrer qu'il les dépasse. Elles avaient beau être hautains, ces tchotchoro du quartier...." (54)[They are just rumta—and Massa Yo was sure he'd bend them to his will! He'd teach them who was in charge! They could be as haughty as they liked, those local kids—the tchotchoro—he knew how to handle them] (*Dog Days*, 36). "Rumta" and "tchotchoro" are synonymous words that could be translated as "girls in their teens." Kouega defines the term 'tchotchoro' as "small, not ripe" (297), and provides the following example to drive home his point: "Mon grand ne tchatche pas avec les tchotchoro nga comme toi" [My elder brother does not chat up small girls like you] (297). The word conveys the extra-linguistic signification of "green horn" or "inexperienced." Nganang's domestication of the French language provides a cultural backdrop for his narrative.

Some code switches in *Temps de chien* introduce elements of vulgarity into the discourse for comic effect. An interesting example is seen in the following passage: "Il se leva sur la pointe des pieds et maudit par-dessus la tête de tout le monde la femme qui avait osé le découvrir en public: Youa mami pima!"(222)[He got up on his tiptoes and, shouting over every one's head, cursed the woman who'd dared to expose him in public: "Youa mami pima!"](*Dog Days*, 154) Kouega(2013) observes that the word 'pima' refers to sexual organs. We need to emphasize that "pima" is the popular word for "vagina." Kouega further observes that the word 'mami pima' is "an insult serious enough to generate a fight"(232). This is because "youa mami pima" is a swear expression that belittles the person at whom it is directed. Literally, it means "your mother's vagina." Another expression that translates sexuality and bears lascivious overtones in *Temps de chien* is "ma din wa" as seen in the following passage: "Je t'ai déjà dit: ma din wa. Je sais que tu n'aimes que l'argent, mais moi je t'aime" (231) [I've already told you, ma din wa, I love you. I know you love money, but I still love you] (*Dog Days*, 161). "Ma din wa" is a Beti language expression which could be translated as "I love you" as the translator indicated in the glossary (208). However, uttered by a whore, the expression would carry ironic undertones because it is devoid of affection given the pecuniary motive behind the love affair. As a matter of fact, Cameroonian prostitutes employ it as a euphemism for "I love your money." Nganang artfully weaves vernacular turns of phrase into his narrative in order to establish a universe of discourse as these examples discussed illustrate.

Temps de chien is an indigenized[43] French language text that becomes less and less standardized and quite often draws from several registers. To translate Mboudjak's actions and interactions with other characters in the novel, his thoughts, in short, the totality of his experience and existence into the written word, Nganang deems it necessary to alternate codes. He effectively uses the interplay of several codes—standard French, English, Pidgin, and indigenous languages—as a stylistic device for not only foregrounding the idiosyncrasies of characters but also for evaluating their relationships to one another.

The foregoing succinct analysis leads to the conclusion that *Temps de chien* is a hybridized text written principally in streetwise French. It is a record of the domesticated French readers would hear in neighbourhoods in principal cities of Cameroon namely Yaounde, Douala, Bafoussam, Garoua, Ngaoundere and more. Nganang's diction and lexical manipulations require readers to be conversant with the localized French spoken in Cameroon. To relish this novelty, the reader has to be not only multilingual but also multicultural. This study enables us to appreciate not just the particular importance Nganang attaches to code-switching as a narrative device but also the cultural hybridity that serves as the backdrop against which his text is written. Whatever amount of success this novel has had, it is primarily on account of the peculiarity of the writer's narrative style—diction and code-switching. By adopting an approach that borders on linguistic miscegenation, Nganang succeeds in forging a style of his own; a canon that enables him to convey

---

[43] For more on linguistic indigenization as a literary canon, read Vakunta's *Indigenization of Language in the African Francophone Novel: A New Literary Canon* (2010).

not only his personal idiolect but also the collective sociolect of the Cameroonian rank and file. In *Temps de chien*, linguistic and extralinguistic factors merge to convey not only the totality of the message intended by the writer but also to delineate the universe of discourse. Situational dimensions and role-shifts call for corresponding code-shifts in order for the reader to interpret the text hermeneutically in order to fully comprehend the holistic message. It is evident from the examples discussed above that Nganang uses code-switching to translate human interest narratives into the written word. His recourse to code-switching is determined by the roles played by characters in different discursive contexts.

It seems as if the novelist resorts to the domestication of the French language as a literary canon for the sole purpose of underscoring the question of intercultural untranslatability, especially when he reverts to loanwords from Cameroonian indigenous languages. However, it would be reductionist to restrict the objective of Nganang's linguistic innovation project to translation per se. We contend in this study that the driving force behind Nganang's linguistic experimentation is the desire to put a high premium on Cameroonian native languages and cultures. The cultural functions of language are critical to the understanding of his text. In our reading of *Temps de chien*, we have been mindful of the function the writer ascribes to vocabulary in context. Without a sound understanding of linguistic contextualization, the significance of Nganang's creative choices would elude the reader.

This study underlines one seminal aspect of literary criticism in African literature. In fictional writing, form is inseparable from content, just as textual information is indissociable from the non-textual. Nganang's narrative technique cannot be dissociated from his ideological interrogations. Quite apart from having an esthetic value, the novel has a psycho-sociological quality reflected in the novelist's use of language—relationship between language, content and context of writing. The significance of this study resides not only in its raising awareness to the problems that fictional writing in hybridized languages may pose to readers and translators but also in its contribution to a deeper understanding of cross-cultural communication, particularly the cultural functions of translation in literature. Potential translation problems have to be addressed in order to make Cameroonian literature written in multiple codes intelligible to global readership. Translation is an activity of enormous importance to the multilingual international community. It is a subject that raises thorny questions for translators of Cameroonian literature; the more so because the peculiarity of contemporary Cameroonian literature is that within it oral traditions coexist with the encroaching print tradition as will become evident in the discourse that constitutes the content of Chapter seven.

Chapter 7

Camfranglais and the Question of Orality in Cameroonian Literature

The context in which Cameroonian literature is written provides evidence to support the claim that when a relatively new cultural system based on the written tradition is superimposed upon an oral tradition, the oral culture does not immediately disappear by the mere fact of its being in contact with the print culture, nor does the "literature" of the oral society vanish on account of the introduction of written literature. The two media coexist and benefit from each other. In the same line of argument, Scheub points out:

> With the advent of literature, the oral tradition did not die. The two media continued their parallel development: both depended on a set of similar narrative and poetic principles, and each proceeded to develop these within its own limits ....There is no unbridgeable gap between them; they constantly nourish each other ("A Review," 16)

Such literary synthesis is feasible insofar as a number of conditions are present at the point of encounter between oral and written traditions, including especially the extent to which the synthesizing artist (the writer) is well rooted in the oral forms of traditional narratives. Obiechina speculates on what would happen in the event that these conditions were present:

A synthesis takes place in which characteristics of the oral culture survive and are absorbed, assimilated, extended, and even re-organized within a new cultural experience. Also, vital aspects of the oral literature are absorbed into an emerging written literature of greatly invigorated forms infused with vernacular energy through metaphors, images and symbols, more complex plots, and diversified structures of meaning.("Narrative Proverbs in the African Novel,"123)

As discussed above, Cameroonian writers make a conscious effort to keep both oral and written traditions in cohesion in works of fiction. In Cameroonian literature there are close ties between oral and written words as the following excerpt from *Moi taximan* illustrates:

"La sagesse des anciens m'apparaissent dans sa nudité étincellante: 'c'est ce qui est dans le ventre qui porte ce qui est sur la tête.'"(19)
[The wisdom of the elders become crystal clear to me: 'it is what you carry in your stomach that sustains what you have in your head.]

This proverbial usage translates not only the modes of speech of elders in Cameroon but also their worldview. It is also a marker of the sagacity of thoughts that comes with age.

Oral tradition cannot be dissociated from the written word in the context of contemporary Cameroonian fiction because the majority of Cameroonians who write are steeped in their indigenous cultures and tend to make use of oral motifs and imagery in literary creativity. Their written works are couched in the manner and style of the traditional oral artist. The reason is that the intent of these writers is to become the 'modern griots' or bards of their societies. An unbroken link has existed between orality and literacy in Cameroonian literature from the earliest times to the present. From time immemorial, Cameroonian literature has been involved in a complex dialogue with the oral tradition, thematically and formally. There is a perceptible interaction between the profoundly rooted oral tradition and the burgeoning literary tradition in Cameroonian literature. There is constant nourishing of the literary tradition by orature, and it is likely that the reverse is true. In other words, written works are built around or grow out of the oral tradition. In this perspective, modern Cameroonian writers owe as much to literacy as they do to orality.

Given that "orality" has been given different labels namely "oral literature," "folk literature," "orature," and "folklore," it would be necessary to settle a few issues relating to the terms used in this study. Okpewho defines oral literature as "literature delivered by word of mouth" (3). He maintains that there are certain techniques which may be used to good effect in oral literature but which may not work in written literature. Conversely, there are certain devices and elements in written literature which may be seen as borrowings or survivals from oral literature. Orature is a recent but seldom used term that emphasizes the oral character of oral literature which comprises riddles, proverbs, epics, myths, chants and songs and more. Folk literature, Okpewho asserts, identifies the creators of this literature as the folk, by which was frequently meant the common, uneducated people mostly in villages or rural communities.

Eno Belinga, on his part, looks at oral literature from the vantage point of esthetics. He puts a premium on the esthetic value of the language of oral literature when he posits: "On peut définir la littérature orale comme, d'une part, l'usage esthétique du langage non écrit et d'autre part, l'ensemble des connaissances et les activités qui s'y rapportent" (7) [Oral literature could be defined as the esthetic use of unwritten language on the one hand, and the sum total of knowledge and related activities on the other.] For the purpose of this study, our definition of oral literature is the same as that of Nandwa and Bukenya who define the term as:

> Those utterances, whether spoken, recited or sung, whose composition and performance exhibit to an appreciable degree the artistic characteristics of accurate observation, vivid imagination and indigenous expression (Quoted in Okpewho, 4-5)

Oral literature is, in essence, dependent on a performer who composes his "text" in words on the spur of the moment. This extemporaneousness is very important in literature composed in Camfranglais. The reason is that Camfranglais is a language in flux. New words and expressions are constantly being added literally on a daily basis. Thus, the connection between composition and transmission is much more intimate in oral literature than is the case in written literature. In Cameroonian oral literature, questions about the means of actual communication are of prime importance. As Finnegan (2007) points out: "Without the oral realization and direct rendition by singer or speaker an unwritten literary piece cannot easily be said to have any continued or independent existence at all" (78).

Unlike Finnegan, Miller defines oral literature in retrospect and perceives orality and literacy to be at variance. As he puts it: "Orality and literacy are two worlds that coexist in a state of tension, enriching and contradicting each other in daily life" (69). Although Miller sees tension in the cohabitation of orality with the written tradition, he, at any rate, sees the mutual enrichment that ensues from the cohabitation between these two literary media. It seems to us, therefore, that the conflict to which he draws our attention is absent in African literature, as he realizes when he elucidates:

> The opposition between orality and literacy in Black Africa is not, however, a clear distinction between, on the one hand, a purely authentic pre-colonial mode of expression preserved intact and, on the other hand, a fully westernized mode undifferentiated from European culture. (71)

Cameroonian literature written in Camfranglais embodies those non-literate forms of expression that sustain the written word. The proximity of oral traditions is one of the distinctive characteristics of Cameroonian oral literature. The critical point to note at this juncture is the fact that contrary to the claims of theorists such as Miller and ilk, there is no rigid dichotomy between oral and written traditions in Cameroonian literature. Assumptions about the identity of orature and its differentiation from literature need to be examined at close range. There are, of course, ways in which oral literature differs somewhat from the written form especially in matters pertaining to its composition and transmission. This notwithstanding, to argue that there is a definite break between these two modes of literary expression is not sustainable. Reasoning with us is Finnegan who observes:

> The two terms are...relative ones, and to assign any given piece unequivocally to either one category or the other—as if they were self-contained and mutually exclusive boxes—can distort the nature of the evidence (Quoted in Stolz and Shannon, 137).

To put this differently, oral and literary traditions comprise relative and overlapping rather than mutually exclusive categories in Cameroonian literature. The view that there is no essential chasm between oral and written literatures is the basic assumption throughout this chapter which aims to dispel the misconception according to which written Cameroonian literature is discontinuous with the oral. Arguing along similar lines, Scheub concludes his "A Review" (1985) with an emphatic statement in support of the view that there is an orality/literacy continuum in African literature:

> There is an unbroken continuity in African verbal art forms, from interacting oral genres to such literary productions as the novel and poetry....The early literary traditions were beneficiaries of the oral genres, and there is no doubt that the epic and its hero are predecessors of the novel and its central characters" (1).

What might be considered "mixed" forms in Cameroonian literature have had a long history—forms that were at some point in time written but have reached their fullest actualization by being performed orally. Examples include the Bamoun religious poems publicly intoned for the enlightenment of the masses; Fulani poems declaimed aloud, and Bamunka compositions memorized as oral poems and chanted by celebrants during marriage ceremonies. Indeed, much of what is normally classified as poetry Cameroonian oral literature is designed to be performed in a musical setting, thus musical and verbal elements are interdependent as seen in Mongo Beti's novel *Perpétue ou l'habitude du malheur* (1974). At first sight, this text may appear to be devoid of elements of orality; however, a closer reading would show that it is indeed shrouded in the folklore of the Beti, especially the novelist's insertion of folktales and myths in the narrative.

Mongo Beti exploits the rich tapestry of the 'Mvett'[44] in order to enrich his novel with the oral traditions of his people. The novel is woven around a homology between Essola Wendelin and the mythical ancestor Akomo Mba whose exploits are chanted via the medium of the 'mvett'. This novel underscores the significance of songs in Beti orature. In Beti traditional communities, songs fulfil special social functions—there are war songs, thrashing songs, marriage songs, drinking songs—songs for all social occasions. The didacticism of some of these songs is non-negligible given the important moral lessons to be learned by the younger generation. Others teach the customs and traditions of the communities to the youths. Such is the essence of the 'mvett'. Mongo Beti taps into the folk tradition of his people for creative writing material. And that is what makes his writing appealing and relevant to his people. As

---

[44]The "mvett" or "mvet" is a musical instrument of the Fang (one of the Beti ethnic groups). It is also a series of stories pertaining to fang warriors often narrated with the accompaniment of music played on this instrument. Beyond the use that was made of this instrument in times of war, the art of the mvett encompasses all aspects of the fang culture. See Tsira Ndong Ndoutoume's *Le Mvett : l'homme, la mort et l'immortalité* (1993)

Nnolim puts it: "...judicious use of the folk tradition is at the root of the appeal of much of the literature emanating from black Africa...." (16) By folk tradition, she means the unrecorded traditions of a people such as their customs, beliefs, magical realism, rituals, myths, legends, and proverbial sayings. *Perpétue ou l'habitude du malheur* speaks with a distinct accent, and voice that parody the Beti oral tale—the mvett. It is clear that anyone who attempts to critique Beti's literary work must do so as a comparatist because this novel has oral antecedents. In other words, Beti constantly draws attention not just to the events being recounted but also to the double-voicedness of his narrative. It is for this reason that Nkosi points out with regard to the African novelist that "His function is to identify the varieties of human experience embodied in each idiom, to note what is vital and what is useful, and where his skills enable him to assist his people in preserving the best from their tradition and absorbing the best from outside" (111). With the vast spread of communication, art is crossing frontiers more rapidly than ever before, each idiom modifying the one with which it comes into contact.

An appreciation of novels written in Camfranglais, including the ones analysed in this book depends on some awareness of the oral material on which the writers draw. We cannot hope to fully comprehend their full impact if we consider only the base words printed on a page. Sadly enough, some critics of African literature seem to lose sight of this subtlety. In *The Singer of Tales* (1960), for example, Lord contends:

> The two techniques [oral and written] are ... contradictory and mutually exclusive. Once the oral

technique is lost, it is never regained. The written technique… is not compatible with the oral technique, and the two could not possibly combine to form another, a third, a transitional technique"(129).

It is misleading to attempt to draw a strict line of demarcation between the verbal arts of literate and non-literate societies as Lord attempts to do in his work. In fact, the case can be made in support of the fact that there is interdependence between oral and written media not only in Cameroonian literature written in Camfranglaish but also in other kinds of Cameroonian literature. Finnegan maintains:

When one looks hard at the detailed circumstances and nature of literary phenomenon in a wide comparative context, historically as well as geographically, the concept of "oral literature" does cease to be a very clear one, because of the varying ways in which a literary piece can be oral (or written): "Orality" is a relative thing (Quoted in Stolz and Shannon, 141).

There certainly is an undeniable overlap of orality and literacy in Cameroonian literature written in Camfranglais as the examples revisited in previous chapters of this book suggest. It is, of course, possible to set a narrower definition of "oral," confining it solely to pieces composed during oral delivery. In principle, there is nothing unfeasible about such an approach. But this sort of reductionist paradigm does little justice to the practical realities of the many different and overlapping forms which literary formulations have taken throughout space and time. Many Cameroonian writers construe literary continuity as a search for a heritage from oral traditions to the new literatures written in European languages. The impression one often gets from the postulations of some scholars (Goody, 1987; Havelock, 1976, 1982; Lord, 1968; Ong, 1982) is that there is something clear-cut and definite called "oral composition." Oral literature is not a clear-cut category, nor is it opposed in any absolute way to written literature. The manner in which orality is embedded in writing makes explicit the cultural imperatives of which the fiction is an effect as Finnegan rightly points out: "The detailed way in which the performer enacts the literary product of his art naturally varies from culture to culture and also among the different literary genres of one language" (*Oral Literature in Africa*, 1970, 5). This observation underlines the importance of "authorship" in Cameroonian literature written in Camfranglais.

The question of authorship remains a moot point in studies addressing the issue of orality in African literature. While some scholars (Belinga, 1965; Finnegan, 1970; Julien, 1992, Okpewho, 1992); Scheub, 1972, 1975, 1977b) agree that oral artists do place a stamp of individuality on their compositions; others maintain that oral literature is a fossilized account of oral tradition passed down from one generation to the next. Foley, for instance, contends:

> If oral literature has taught us anything, it is that authorship as we know it in the modern era does not exist in oral tradition....Poets composing written materials by means of the oral traditional method—owe a great deal of what we call an "authorship" to the generations of traditional poets who preceded them. The instrument of oral traditional phraseology, for instance, as highly patterned and formulaic as it is, was shaped not by a

single artist or group of artists, but rather by the sum of the many individuals involved in verse-making over the decades and centuries before the semi-observable event of the text that survives to us. (8)

Persuasive as this reasoning may be, it needs to be pointed out that oral literature is not the common property of joint or communal authorship. Indeed, each version of an oral tale bears the stamp of character and narrative technique peculiar to its narrator. Finnegan's comments on Limba storytellers in her *Limba Stories and Storytelling* (1967) buttress this fact:

> The storytellers [among the Limba of Sierra Leone] are all individuals, individuals who perform on specific occasions. There is no joint common 'folk' authorship or set form of performance dictated by blind tradition. The stories are, naturally, composed and enacted within the limits of the social background of Limba life and literary conventions; but each individual performer has their own idiosyncrasies and unique fund of experience, interests and skills. (17)

Thus, we find ourselves at a linguistic crossroads in Cameroonian literature written in Camfranglais. Each individual writer borrows from the font of Camfranglais lexicon. However, each borrowed word is given a contextualized signification depending on the social provenance of the creative writer. Bamileke fiction writers like Nganang and Fonkou write Camfranglais with Bamileke connotations; Beti fiction writers like Fouda write Camfranglais with connotations culled from the Beti group of languages. This holds true for Bassa creative writers who embellish Camfranglais with words and expressions gleaned from Bassa language. As we strive to unravel the truth about this ideological conundrum, it is imperative to interrogate how oralization and orally-derived texts generate meaning. Part of what Finnegan implies when she portrays Limba storytellers as individuals who perform on specific occasions is that in a community setting where two or more storytellers tell the same stories, one version of a tale is bound to differ from another version, depending not only on the narrator's personal virtuosity and expertise at improvisation but also on the context, notably the type of audience to whom the tale is narrated. The contemporary novel in Cameroon written in Camfranglais represents, one would suggest, the mediation between the tradition of orality and Western narrative conventions as formalized in written texts. Irele (2001) observes that the novel "integrates the formal properties of imaginative expression in both the African and Western registers" (85). We are dealing in this context with two levels of mediation: first, between the oral text as received and recorded in its original language of delivery and its reformulation in the European language, and the written text of the published version. The two mediations are then intensified by subsidiary devices which, according to Irele, contribute to the formal pattern and the scheme of reference of the work .Within the space of a written text in a European language, the Cameroonian writer incorporates the essential elements of the oral narrative at significant points in his/her works in order to reflect their appropriateness to situations and for special effects.

The narratives in the Cameroonian texts discussed above are spiced with aphorisms, proverbs, warnings, and praise-words, functioning to alert the reader as to how to read the events. These verbal cues serve as pointers to the cultural contexts in which the narratives take place and as devices the purpose of which is to add lustre to the drab tone of realistic textual development as seen in other texts by Mongo Beti. Beti's *Mission terminée* (1957) has been described by some critics as a parody of the Cameroonian Mvet. Beti has not hesitated to resort to popular vocabulary or onomatopoeia, considered as a sort of oral punctuation. He does not invent, he translates. His novel *Remember Ruben* (1980) could be viewed as a palimpsest of Cameroonian oral traditions on account of its being grafted on Beti folklore. Allusions to the novel's epic dimensions are evident in the narrator's comparison of the protagonists' ordeal to the adventures of the protagonist in Homer's epic poem *Odyssey*: "Il nous faudra attendre vingt ans pour connaître enfin, bribe par bribe, l'odyssée digne d'Akomo, vécue par les deux plus admirables enfants d'Ekoumdom" (83).[We have to wait twenty years to learn, little by little, of the Odyssey, worthy of Akomo himself, lived by the two most admirable sons of Ekoumdoum] (*Remember Ruben*, 64-5). The epic proportions of this novel and its sequel *La ruine presque cocasse d'un polichinelle* (1979) are attributable to the preponderance of valiant acts in the narrative, the big battles fought by the protagonist Mor-Zamba and his companions against forces that far outmarch them but who come out victorious ultimately on account of their astuteness and perseverance. One cannot help but recognize Beti's dexterity in calquing his novel on existing ethno-texts. The feat achieved by him resides in his success in merging oral tradition with the exigencies of modernist literary creativity. His style does not only approximate oral performance; it amounts to an appropriation of the intrinsic values of oral tradition for an imaginative purpose in written literature.

Francis Bebey emulates Beti's style in his own novels. A dominant characteristic of Bebey's narrative technique is polytonality (also called multi-voicedness). His style produces a form of expression that is akin to the folktale of traditional Douala storytellers. Like the traditional storyteller Bebey knows how to captivate his readers and excite their curiosity by toying with their emotions, by withholding vital information and by posing tantalizing questions. Like Beti, Bebey anticipates the presence of a live audience. There are several interpolative remarks in *Le fils d'Agatha Moudio* (1967) that give the reader the impression that the narrator imagines himself to be in the company of an audience. For example, the narrator addresses himself directly to the reader: "Ecoutemoi, et réponds-moi... (104)[Listen and answer me...] (*Agatha Moudio's Son*, 77).

It should be noted that the key word here is "listen," for his tale is supposed to be listened to in much the same way as members of the audience would listen to a tale told under the village palaver tree[45] at the end of a day of hard labor on the farm. Some of these interjections are, indeed, directed at readers, individually and collectively. Other interpolations

---

[45] In Africa, the "palaver tree" refers to the sacred baobab tree under which village elders meet to exchange ideas. Beneath this tree misunderstandings are resolved and critical community issues are discussed under the direction of the elders. Villagers explain points of view and together, through group consensus reach a final decision. But the palaver tree stands for more than group discussions and problem-solving; it is the place of the festivals, the harvest celebration and where the traveling storyteller sets up his camp in the evening to spin the tales of a place and time far off and free from the worries of rural farming. See Jacques Chevrier's *L'arbre à palabres* (2005).

such as "croyez-moi…" (67)[Believe me…] (*Agatha Moudio's Son*, 77) serve as reassurances for the listener's supposed reactions to what the narrator says. It is through oralization that the reader of *Le fils d'Agatha Moudio* experiences the shape and sound of oral performance. The exclamatory and interrogative moods the novelist uses contribute to the sustenance of a dynamic relationship between the narrator and the narratee.

Bebey's narrator frequently appeals for our attention. At times, he calls for our patience. He even whets our appetite. Intercalations like these affirm the dynamic relationship between audience and narrator as well as the latter's tight control over the act of storytelling. Bebey believes that by wedding the style of the traditional storyteller with the Western style of novelistic writing, he produces something rather unique. What emerges from this Cameroonian writer's experimentation with stylistics is a novel irrigated by a dual tradition—African and Western. In an interview he granted Norman Stokle on August 20, 1977, Bebey expatiates on the creative transposition process that takes place in his literary works:

> I rely heavily on the musicians in my country who play the mvet and tell stories with it. From time to time, they launch into lengthy poetic descriptions about the forest or whatever. And sometimes, they start speaking as though they were a double personality, two people speaking to each other ….There is no transition between the art of narrating and that of singing or playing music. For me, it's all the same world. I never knew of any musician back

home who didn't tell stories or recite poems. All of the arts blend together as a unity(110)[46]

The merging of oral storytelling and the written word is evident in Bebey's second novel *Le roi Albert d'Effidi* (1976) The witty digressions, quips and lyrical flights characteristic of the narrator's discourse in this novel are the hallmarks of the mvet storyteller. Like the mvet storyteller, Bebey's narrator combines comedy, farce and witticism together in his attempt to portray traditional African life. His point of reference is the local "griot-conteur" with whose narrative tricks his is thoroughly familiar. His frame of reference is one in which the telling of a tale is a social event to be relished by the entire community.

Like all good storytellers Bebey is a master of the word, endowed with a good sense of humor, and a predilection for irony and sarcasm of which he makes effective use in order to

---

[46]Francis Bebey is musician-cum-writer. Born in Douala-Cameroon, he grew up surrounded by music from an early age. His father, a protestant minister, taught him to sing. He brought his son up listening to classical music from the Western world, but the young boy was also closely in touch with his African roots, soaking up traditional melodies from his homeland. African music was his overriding passion. Bebey started out mastering the art of the banjo but later abandoned the instrument in favor of the guitar. Committed to preserving the essence of his traditional music heritage, Bebey made sparing use of electric instruments, preferring to put the emphasis on traditional instruments such as the Pygmy flute and the *sanza* (thumb piano). In 1968, he performed his first Paris concert at the American Center, presenting a multi-lingual repertoire (in Duala, French and English) inspired by traditional Bantu songs and polyphonic Pygmy music. To meet Bebey is to meet an eclectic mind. On May 28, 2001, the global music community lost one of its greatest performers when Bebey died of a heart attack at his Paris home. For more on Bebey, see his work *African Music: A People's Art* (1975).

uphold oral tradition and to entertain the audience/reader. It is probably for this reason that Stokle notes that "... the Africanization of the novel in Bebey's hands has resulted in the 'griotization' of the narrator ... and it is here that we discern certain flaws in Bebey's technique" (111). Though we are in agreement with Stokle's contention that Bebey employs the European language to animate the African scene, we find it hard to espouse his view that the 'griotization' of oral narrative in Bebey's novels is tantamount to a literary flaw. On the contrary, his recourse to indigenization enriches the African novel. The griot is the symbol of orality in African literatures and there is no better way of underscoring the oral texture of an African text than bringing the griot into the limelight. Bebey himself is quite explicit on the essence of the cultural hybridity that serves as the unifying force in his fictional writing: "Whether I replace French by Duala is not the point. What matters is that I extract the essence of Duala and put it alongside the essence of French so as to attain a much enriched cultural level. It is not a technical problem but a cultural one..." (Quoted in Stokle, 112)

Bebey's novels could be seen as a creative reworking of traditional oral tales, a palimpsestical reproduction of ethno-texts. His close adherence to the speech mannerisms, worldview, and thought-patterns of the Duala traditional storytellers assigns to his work an aura of nativity that crystallizes his African consciousness. In this light, it is relevant to point out that it is only when one acknowledges the continuum in the continent's verbal arts; when one dismantles the supposed wall between orality and the written tradition, when one discovers the ancient roots of the African novel that one becomes aware of the richness of this art tradition.

The foregoing observations buttress the claim that oral literature has distinctive characteristics: themes, techniques, and perspectives. Mazisi Kunene notes that oral literature "is a literature which is not frozen, not put in the book, not intended for a particular category of people" (5). The way in which orality is embedded in Cameroonian fictional writing makes explicit the historical and cultural imperatives of which the fiction is an effect. Cameroonian literature could be deemed to comprise a body of "texts" constituting not merely a repertoire of verbal art forms, with established conventions for composition and transmission, but also a body of written texts with canons in the strict sense of the word. The fact of a direct progression from orality to literacy is crucial in this chapter which upholds the view that the perception of creative writing needs to transcend the simplistic notion of drawing upon material from folklore, and fully embrace the devices through which such material is manipulated through writing to give expression to forms that already exist in indigenous languages. The predominance of orality as a shaping medium is a determinant in the process through which such material is recreated and brought to a new mode of existence through the written word. In Cameroonian literature, oral narrative strategies tend to be conventionalized for use in the written tradition.

We find in Cameroonian literature an imaginative centering of the traditional society and culture in terms of both thematic and structural paradigms. The result is that within the very form of expression of the contemporary Cameroonian writer, there is a blending of oral and Western literary traditions. The connection between orality and literacy functions as a locus of consciousness and as a reference for self-identification. Irele (2001) makes the point that "what gives interests to the literary situation today in Africa is the way our written literature, in both the indigenous languages and the European languages, enacts dialectic between orality and literacy" (38).

It should be noted that Cameroonian writers are not under duress to evoke orality in their fictional works. They do so only because they elect to do so. It is a conscious act of creative translation intended to convey concepts that may defy expression in European languages as seen in this example taken from Fonkou's *Moi taximan*: "Justine sortait de ses cours. Nous effectuions le trajet habituel. Elle me laissa vider mon sac. Elle ne dit rien tout de suite, comme si ma proposition ne l'avait pas surprise" (132) [Justine was returning from class. We had taken the usual route. She allowed me empty my bag. She did not respond immediately as if she was not surprised at my proposal.] The expression "vider mon sac" may disconcert a non-Cameroonian reader of Fonkou's novel because it is an indigenized French expression calqued on mother tongue turns of phrase which could be translated into English as "speak one's mind." The question of integrating oralized verbal structures into written literature has generated intense and somewhat controversial debate among critics of African literature. Tine, for instance, maintains: "La littérature africaine se définit comme une littérature située entre l'oralité et l'écriture. Cette idée a permis la réalisation d'un vaste consensus qui va des critiques africanistes aux écrivains" (99) [African literature can be defined as a literature that straddles orality and literacy. This idea has given rise to a vast consensus between African critics and authors.]

We find Tine's implied bias toward a literary "purgatory" for African writers rather intriguing. It is disingenuous to claim that African oral literature is at an embryonic stage of its evolution toward the written form, as Tine seems to suggest. Interestingly, Julien(1992)seems to subscribe to Tine's view of a "redemptive stage" in African literature when she observes: "Orality is ...viewed as a precious good threatened by writing, but one that nonetheless will or must be distilled and preserved inside it"(22). Cameroonian literature is none of the above. Creative writing in Cameroonian could best be described as hybrid literature emanating from the dual use of oral and written modes of expression. This blended literary creativity is attributable to the fact that one of the essential characteristics of Cameroonian cultures is orality. Cameroonian writers tend to be purveyors of indigenous cultures—their oral traditions are in them and inform their works. To be able to use stories that have been extrapolated from the oral traditional repertory requires that the fiction writer be well grounded in the art of storytelling. The absolute pre-condition for integrating folk stories in written literature is an awareness of the technique of literary transposition, given that what matters is not the story itself but how well it is transposed into the written medium. The written code imposes considerable constraints on the writer, the more so because paralinguistic features such as facial expressions, bodily movements, voice pitches, and more are necessarily reduced, if not eliminated altogether in the written text.

The most striking example of oralization in the Cameroonian novel written in Camfranglais is the use of proverbial expressions. Proverbs are tired clichés only when viewed in isolation, but when they are placed into realistic contexts, they become vital, even dynamic as seen in this example from Fonkou's *Moi taximan*: "Nos patrons n'ignorent pas que la fourmi peut tuer un elephant, ni que les termites renversent de grandes cases"(15) [Our bosses are not unaware of the fact that an ant is capable of killing an elephant, or that termites can fell a big house.] This is a weighty proverb that serves as a warning to oppressors. The literary relevance of narrative proverbs in Cameroonian literature is incontestable, as they are a rich source of imagery. In Cameroonian cultures a feeling for imagery and for the expression of abstract notions through compressed and allusive phraseology comes out particularly clearly in the use of proverbs. Proverbial expressions establish fresh ties with the writer's culture. They provide cultural and artistic life to fiction. Even a cursory reading of *Moi taximan* would reveal that each proverb brings something new and refreshing to the total meaning of the story. Fonkou's proverbs bring new insight to the narrative—they clarify the action, sharpen characterization, elaborate themes and, enrich the setting of the action. Most importantly, proverbs help to define the epistemological contours of the novel: the reader is made to become aware that the narrative context is oral, that within it, knowledge is attained through analogy, allusion, and metaphoric extension. The use of the narrative proverb in the structuring of action in the novel is a major constructional strategy in the expression of oral traditional impulse in the lives of characters and in defining their vernacular sensibility. Orality in *Moi taximan* is more than a stylistic intrusion; it is the means by which Fonkou achieves the poetics of verisimilitude and factual portrayal of experience.

As these examples show, proverbs, myths, riddles, legends, chants and folktales are used as subtexts in Cameroonian works of fiction. In this perspective, contemporary Cameroonian literature could be seen as a weak imitation of these ethno-texts. The narrative proverb, in particular, could be construed as a text in itself because it is often made to serve an extended function in literature. By resorting to proverbs, Cameroonian writers draw attention to the centrality of figurative language as a mode of expression in indigenous speech. The use of proverbs in Cameroonian literature is not in itself a distinguishing feature, given that proverbs are used in fiction in other world literatures. However, what makes proverbial usage in Cameroonian literature peculiar is their functionality. As Obiechina points out:

> All these are assimilated to the form and give it distinctive qualities of its own, penetrating and transforming its structure and extending its scope and making it a dynamic vehicle for exploring historical, social, cultural, political, and psychological themes, for articulating human problems and dilemmas and for raising and integrating consciousness (138).

It is often difficult to unravel the latent meanings of proverbs, also called ethno-texts, without some knowledge of the cultural backdrop against which the expressions are used as well as the significations conveyed by the signifiers. For example, the meaning of the following Zulu proverb would be lost to a non-Zulu reader who has no knowledge of Zulu customs and mores: "No proud girl ever had the better of the skin-skirt" (Finnegan, 1970, 406). The meaning of this saying would remain undecipherable if the reader were unaware of the fact that only married women wear skin-skirts in Zulu culture. Finnegan notes that this proverb refers to the tonic effect that marriage has on proud cheeky Zulu girls. The irrefutable interplay between orality and literacy in African works of fiction demolishes the rigid line of demarcation which some literary critics seek to establish between oral and written traditions. The dichotomy disappears because as Obiechina maintains, "it does not accommodate the poetics of narrative synthesis in which oral and literate narrative forms and styles infuse" (125).

In this chapter, we have sought to challenge and dispel the misconception that Cameroonian written literature is discontinuous with the oral. The foregoing discourse leaves us with no doubt that contemporary Cameroonian literature written in Camfranglais is a hybrid form of writing in which orality and literacy co-exist to be mutually sustaining. The two modes of storytelling constantly draw on the products of the other; orally transmitted forms are frequently adopted and adapted in the written form, and written literature too draws on oral sources. It is misleading as well as futile, to attempt to establish a profound and unbridgeable rift between traditional verbal art forms on the one hand, and written literatures on the other. Oral literature is only one kind of literature, a type of storytelling characterized by particular features, namely performance, transmission and audience participation. But for all these differences, the postulate in this book is that of continuity between oral and print traditions in Cameroonian fictional writing in which there is no essential line of demarcation between the two modes of expression. The constant interplay between the spoken and the written word reflects features that belong in the oral and literary traditions. The blending of both traditions gives Cameroonian literature its unique character as a hybridized form of writing. Cameroonian writers' intent to replicate their cultural substrata subsumed in oral tales often determines the stylistic choices they must make in the writing process. In the chapter that follows we intend to provide the reader with a synopsis of the various points of convergence and divergence adumbrated in the preceding chapters of this book.

Chapter 8

Conclusion

It is deemed it appropriate to close this study with an excerpt from Lise Gauvain's seminal work *L'écrivain francophone à la croisée des langues* (1991). This work addresses the linguistic dilemma in which Francophone writers find themselves in the creative writing process:

> Si chaque écrivain doit jusqu'à un certain point réinventer la langue, la situation des écrivains francophones hors de France a ceci d'exemplaire que le français n'est pas pour eux un acquis mais plutôt le lieu et l'occasion de constantes mutations et modifications. Engagés dans le jeu des langues, ces écrivains doivent créer leur propre langue d'écriture, et cela dans un contexte culturel multilingue, souvent affecté des signes de la diglossie (Gauvain (5).
>
> [If, up to a certain point, each writer has to re-invent language, the situation of Francophone writers residing out of France is peculiar in that for them, French is not an acquisition; rather it is an occasion for constant mutations and modifications. Engaged as they are, in the game of language, these writers have to create their own language of fiction, in a multilingual cultural context often affected by signs of diglossia.]

This excerpt provides a cryptic synopsis of the problematic of language in contemporary Cameroonian Francophone literature. Fictional writing in a multilingual context such as Cameroon harbors wide-ranging ramifications for creative writers who tend to bestride linguistic divides in an attempt to infuse fictional works with the particularities of indigenous cultures. Cameroonian writers of French expression constantly resort to the technique of linguistic miscegenation in a bid to transpose their perceptions of reality into French. The thrust of our argument in this book revolves around the assertion that francophone Cameroonian writers are at the crossroads of languages, straddling cultural spaces to articulate that which Gauvain refers to as "la surconscience linguistique de l'écrivain" (6) [the writer's linguistic subconscious]. Our study of the various mechanisms through which code-switching serves as a creative writing modus operandi in the novels discussed above has led us to delve into the functionalism of linguistic appropriation and the role it plays in literary expressivity.

We maintain that Cameroonian writers resort to camfranglais in different contexts for the purpose of projecting group cohesion, social identity and the artefacts of indigenous cultures. By resorting to different domesticating strategies—code switching, semantic shift, compounding, reduplication and more—these novelists create hybrid texts that demand of readers to be not just bilingual but also bicultural. A problematizing of language and narrative paradigms is central to our reading of the works of Fouda, Fonkou, Beti, Bebey, and Nganang. In the full range of their use of language, these writers pay particular attention to both the conscious and subconscious blending of languages, cultures and texts. The contextual function of language is critical to the full understanding of *Je parle camerounais (2001)*, *Moi taximan*(2001) *Temps de chien(2001)*, *Le fils d'Agatha moudio*(1967) *Le roi Albert d'Effidi*(1976), *Mission terminée*(1957) *Remember Ruben*(1980), *Perpétue ou l'habitude du malheur*(1974), *La ruine presque cocasse d'un polichinelle*(1979) and *Branle-bas en noir et blanc* (1999). In our reading of the corpus, we have been mindful of the function ascribed to vocabulary in context and translation in literature Without a full appreciation of linguistic contextualization and the intralingual translation that sustains creative writing in Cameroon, the significance of the plots, characterization and themes discussed in these fictional works would elude the reader.

This book raises the question of the interplay between standard and colloquial language usages, indigenous and imperial languages, and orality versus literacy in contemporary Cameroonian literature. We contend that the contemporary Cameroonian novel of French expression is distinct from its metropolitan counterpart mainly in its being written through the medium of domesticated French. Though written, the novelistic genre in Cameroon remains distinctive in its attachment to the oral traditions of the local people and the specificity of these traditions in contradistinction to European cultures. To fully appreciate the impact of the experiences and socio-cultural realities conveyed in the Cameroonian novel, readers have to be conversant with the traditional verbal art forms that gave rise to the novelistic genre, the more so because Cameroonian writers tend to draw from the font of indigenous languages and cultures in the writing process.

This study makes significant contributions to scholarship in Francophone literary studies. First, it brings to the limelight the rich contribution of Camfranglais, indigenous languages, and Cameroonian Pidgin English to the corpus of literary works written in Cameroon. Secondly, our work explores emerging trends in the evolution of the Cameroonian novel at the level of innovation in language usage. It views positively the project of African writers who are inclined to decolonize national literatures by domesticating the language of the ex-colonizer in a bid to give voice to the ex-colonized. Thirdly, the findings of this study bring useful insights to the concept of linguistic miscegenation, text typology and the need for a suitable framework for the translation of literary texts written in hybridized languages. Fourthly, this book views the pragmatics of translation from an entirely new perspective. Hitherto, translation has been perceived as an interlingual text replacement process whereby the text processor replaces textual material in the source language with equivalent textual material in the target language.

Without undermining the importance of this aspect of translation in international communication, our study sheds ample light on another phase of the translation process—intralingual translation—that which deals with semantic shifts and the transposition of worldview and imagination within the same language. Last but not least, this work makes a substantive contribution to the field of applied linguistics in that it sheds ample light on the literary significance of relexification, reduplication, semantic shifts, code-switching, syntactic fusion, neologisms, diglossia & heteroglossia, dialectization, creolization, pidginization, and other forms of language mixing strategems. This book puts a premium on the need for a multidimensional framework necessary for engaging in literary criticism in the Cameroonian context.

A succinct study of seminal novels in this work reveals that linguistic appropriation constitutes the single most effective tool with which Cameroonian writers indigenize the use of the French language. This book provides evidence to buttress the argument according to which Cameroonian novelistic writing continues to be impacted by the oral traditions and indigenous languages and cultures of the writers. For these writers, creative writing necessitates a continuous interplay between French and indigenous languages. The novels of Nganang, Fouda, Beti, Bebey and Fonkou are imprints of the oral traditions of their respective native cultures. We have attempted to show in the course of this study that the language used in writing the novels analysed is de-Europeanized French characterized by lexical manipulation and Cameoonianisms that amount to what Ouédraogo refers to as "concubinage linguistique" (127) or linguistic concubinage. Stylistic choices made by the aforementioned novelists owe more to their intent to transpose their worldview, speech mannerism and cultural sensibilities into French than to their feeling of discomfort with the French language. The need to de-colonize Cameroonian literature seems to be a major preoccupation of writers under scrutiny in this book.

Whether or not Fouda, Fonkou, Beti, Bebey and Nganang have succeeded in their task of de-Europeanizing the Cameroonian novel of French expression is a moot point. Literary scholars like Ngugi wa Thiong'o argue that to qualify as African literature, writers must write in indigenous languages. Ngugi further argues that "Literature written by Africans in European languages...can only be termed Afro-European literature; that is, literature written by Africans in European languages" (27). Much as we salute the success of the aforementioned novelists in imprinting their texts with the modes of speech characteristic of Cameroonians, we cannot lose sight of the fact their texts are not written in indigenous languages; rather they are written in French, a European language.

In spite of the significant lexical manipulations evident in the novels analysed in preceding chapters, it is still an essentially French lexicon that these writers have used in the writing process. Worse still, glottophagia[47] is a two-way traffic in these texts. While French words have acquired new significations, several indigenous language words have been foreignized in the writing process. For Fouda, Fonkou, Beti, Bebey and Nganang the French language is a necessary evil with which they have come to terms. These writers are in love with both French and their respective mother tongues. Language, whether we consider it from the standpoint of its treatment or the problems created by translating lived experiences into a language that did not shape that reality and was not shaped by it, remains one of the most controversial aspects of the novels we have examined in this book. This gray area calls for in-depth investigation.

Avenues for further research include a multidimensional study of Ivorian *Nouchi*, a counsin *of Camfranglais*. The implementation of the analytical framework used in this study beyond the boundaries of Francophone Africa is likely to engender unexpected outcomes. In particular, a wider application of this paradigm to Kenyan *Sheng*, Sierra Leonian *Krio* and Cape-Verdian creole, is likely to yield surprising findings. A study of francophone literatures of the Americas,

---

[47] According to Chantal Zabus, the term 'glottophagia' was first introduced by Louis-Jean Calvet in *Linguistique et colonialisme* (1974) to refer to the linguistic colonization of Africa" (17). Glottophagy, another name for glottophagia) is a process that affects speech communities where the level of linguistic competence that speakers possess of a given language variety is decreased, eventually resulting in no native or fluent speakers of the variety.

the Pacific, Europe, and the Caribbean would be a rewarding investigation. A study of the works of Creole-speaking Francophone Caribbeans, namely Edouard Glissant, Patrick Chamoiseau, Raphaël Confiant, Jean Bernabé, Jacques Romain and a host of others would be insightful. Like Africans, Caribbean writers consider themselves to be at the crossroads of languages and their texts are emblematic of the linguistic dualism that we have seen in the corpus studied in this book. An in-depth study of Glissant's concept of 'antillanité' (1981) as well as the theory of 'créolité' propounded by Bernabé and peers (1993) in the light of manifestations in prose narratives would be an interesting area into which scholars could delve. Furthermore, it would be insightful to look at how postcolonial writers other than Francophone, notably Anglophone and Lusophone African writers have attempted to transpose the imprint of their cultural backgrounds into fictional writing through linguistic hybridization. An examination of the works of Canadian writer Nadine Bismuth and Nigerian literary giant, Chinua Achebe would be a rewarding literary venture.

The foregoing textual analysis of Cameroonian novels written in Camfranglais reveals one truth about linguistic appropriation: the domestication of language in literature raises intriguing questions and invites new modes of literary criticism. In the introduction to a translation of Martin Buber's *I and Thou* (1970), Kaufmann observes that readers need to feel addressed by the books they read, as if the writer were speaking directly to them. This attitude is required of the reader of the Cameroonian francophone text as well, the more so because "le texte tel qu'il s'écrit aujourd'hui en espace francophone est une traversée des langues et une interrogation sur la fonction du langage" (Gauvin, 14) [the text such as it is written today in the Francophonie zone is a mosaic of languages and an interrogation of the function of language.]

Works cited

Achebe, Chinua. *Things Fall Apart*. London: Heinemann, 1958.

_____. *No longer at Ease*. London: Heinemann, 1960.

_____. *A Man of the People*. London: Heinemann, 1966.

_____. *Morning Yet on Creation Day: Essays*. London: Heinemann, 1975.

Adendorff, Rajend . *"Fanakalo—A Pidgin in South Africa." Language in South Africa*. Cambridge: Cambridge University Press, 2002.

Ambanasom, Shadrach. *The Cameroonian Novel of English Expression: An Introduction*. Bamenda: Langaa RPCIG, 2009.

Asante, M.K. *Afrocentricity*. Trenton: Africa World Press. Paris: Stock, 1988.

Ashuntantang, B. Joyce. *Landscaping Postcoloniality: The Dissemination of Cameroon Anglophone Literature*. Bamenda : Langaa RPCIG, 2009.

Ayafor, Isaiah, Munang. "Official Bilingualism in Cameroon: Instrumental or Integrative Policy?" In 'Proceedings of the 4th International Symposium on Bilingualism'. Ed. James Cohen et al., Somerville: Cascadilla Press, 2005.

Aschcroft, Bill. *Post-colonial Transformation*. London: Routledge, 2001.

Ashcroft, Bill, Gareth Griffiths, Helen Tiffin. Eds. *The Empire Writes Back: Theory and Practice in Post-colonial Literatures*. London and New York: Routledge, 1989.

Badday, Moncef S. "Ahmadou Kourouma, écrivain ivoirien." *L'Afrique littéraire et Artistique 10* (1970): 8-19.

Bandia, P. "Translation as Culture Transfer: Evidence from African Creative Writing," *Traduction, Terminologie, Rédaction*6-2(1993): 55-78.

_____. "On Translating Pidgins and Creoles in African Literature," *Traduction, Terminologie, Rédaction* 6-2, (1993): 94-114.

Bardolph, Jacqueline. *Etudes postcoloniales et littérature.* Paris: Champion, 2002.

Bebey, Francis. *Le fils d'Agatha Moudio.* Yaoundé: Editions CLE, 1967.

_____. *Agatha Moudio's Son.* Trans. Joyce Hutchison A. New York, 1967.

_____. *Le roi Albert d'Effidi.* Yaoundé: Editions CLE, 1976.

Begoechea, Manuel. *Discours et écritures dans les sociétés en mutation.* Paris: L'Harmattan, 2007.

Bjornson, Richard. *A Bibliography of Cameroonian Literature.* Texas : University of Texas Press, 1986.

_____*The African Quest for Freedom and Identity : Cameroonian Writing and the National Experience.* Indianapolis: Indiana University Press, 1991.

Bernabé, Jean, Patrick Chamoiseau and Raphaël Confiant, eds. *Eloge de la créolité.* Paris: Gallimard, 1993.

Beti, Mongo. *Mission terminée.* Paris: Corrêa, 1957.

_____.*Le pauvre Christ de Bomba.* Paris: R. Laffont, 1956.

_____. *Mission to Kala.* Trans. Peter Green. London: F. Muller, 1958.

_____. *Perpétue et l'habitude du malheur.* Paris: Buchet, 1974.

_____. *Perpetua and the Habit of Unhappiness.* Trans. John Reed and Clive Wake. London: Heinemann, 1978.

_____. *La ruine presque cocasse d'un polichinelle.* Paris: Editions des Peuples Noirs, 1979.

_____. *Lament for an African Pol.* Trans. Richard Bjornson. Washington, D.C.: Three Continent Press, 1985.

_____. *Remember Ruben.* Paris: L'Harmattan, 1982.

_____. *Remember Ruben.* Trans. Gerald Moore. London: Heinemann, 1980.

_____.*Trop de soleil tue l'amour.* Paris, Julliard, 1999.

_____.*Branle-bas en noir et blanc.* Paris, Julliard, 2000.

Bhabha, Homi K. *Nation and Narration.* London: Routledge, 1990.

_____. "The Third Space." Ed. Jonathan Rutherford. *Identity: Community, Culture and Difference.* London: Lawrence and Wishart, 1990.

_____. *The Location of Culture.* London: Routledge, 2004.

Biloa, E. "Structure phrastique du Camfranglais: Etat de la question." In Echu, G. & Grundstrom. A.W. Eds. *Official Bilingualism and Linguistic Communication in Cameroon.* New York: Peter Lang, 1999.

Bismuth, Nadine. *Les gens fidèles ne font pas les nouvelles.* Montreal: Boreal, 2001.

Boni, Nazi. *Crépuscule des temps anciens.* Paris: Présence Africaine, 1962.

Botwe-Asamoah, Kwame. "African literature in European Languages: Implications for a Living Literature." *Journal of Black Studies* 31.6 (2001): 746-760.

Buber, Martin. *I and You*. Trans. Walter Kaufmann. New York : Simon and Schuster, 1970.

Calvet, Jean. *Une ou des normes? Insécurité linguistique et normes endogènes en Afrique francophone*. Paris: CIRLFA, 1998.

_____.*La guerre des langues et les politiques linguistiques*. Paris: Payot, 1987.

_____.*Linguistique et colonialisme; petit traité de glottophagie*. Paris: Payot, 1974.

_____. *La littérature français à l'étranger*. Paris: Payot, 1923.

Césaire, Aimé. *Cahier d'un retour au pays natal*. Paris: Présence Africaine, 1956.

_____. *Return to my Native Land*. Trans. Emil Synders. Paris: Présence Africaine, 1968.

_____. *Une tempête*. *Paris :* Editions du Seuil, 1969.

_____.*A Tempest*. New York: TCG Translations, 2002.

Chamoiseau. Patrick. *Chemin d'école*. Paris: Gallimard, 1994.

_____. *Texaco*. Paris : Gallimard, 1992.

Chevrier, Jacques. "Conditions et limites de l'oralité dans l'écriture africaine." *Kompartistische Hefte* 1(1980): 61-66.

_____. "L'écrivain africain devant la langue française." *L'Afrique Littéraire et Artistique* 50 (1978): 47-52.

_____. *L'arbre à palabres*. Paris: Editions Hatier International, 2005.

Chia. E. "Cameroon Home Languages." In Koenig E.L., Chia E. and Povey J. Eds. *A Sociolinguistic Profile of Urban Center s in Cameroon*. Los Angeles: Cross Road Press, 1983.

Chia E. and Gerbault. "Les nouveaux parlers urbains: Le cas de Yaoundé." In Chaudenson, R. *Actes du colloque*

international sur des langues et des villes. Paris: ACCT and Didier Erudition, 1990.
Chinweizu et al. *Toward the Decolonization of African Literature*. Washington D.C.: Howard University Press, 1983.
Confiant, Raphaël, Patrick Chamoiseau, and Jean Bernabé. *In Praise of Creoleness*, Baltimore: The John Hopkins University Press, 1990.
Dadié, Bernard. *Climbié*. Paris: Serghers, 1956.
Derrida, Jacques. "Des Tours de Babel." *Difference in Translation*. Ed and trans. Joseph F. Graham.Itaca: Cornell University Press, 1985.
Dibussi, Tande. "The Yondo Black Affair: Catalyst for Multiparty Politics In Cameroon." Retrieved February 7, 2013 from http://www.dibussi.com/2006/04/the-yondo-black.html
Dingemanse, Mark. "Folk Definitions of Ideophones." Eds. Elizabeth Norcliffe and N.J. Enfield. *Field Manual*Vol.13 (2010): 24-29.
Dingwaney, Anuradha. *Between Languages and Cultures: Translation and Cross-Cultural Texts*. Pittsburgh: University of Pittsburgh, 1995.
Doh, Emmanuel F. *Shadows*. Bamenda: Langaa RPCIG, 2011.
_____. *Oriki'badan*. Bamenda: Langaa RPCIG, 2009.
_____. *The Fire Within*. Bamenda: Langaa RPCIG, 2008.
_____. *Not yet Damascus*. Bamenda: Langaa RPCIG, 2007.
Douglas, D. "Wrestling with Context in Interlanguage Theory." In *Applied Linguistics* 6 (1985): 190-204.
Echu, George. "Influence of Cameroon Pidgin English on the English and Cultural Development of the French

Language" (1991). Retrieved on March 12, 2014 from https://www.indiana.edu/~iulcwp/pdfs/03-echu03.pdf

_____. "Pidginization of French in Cameroon" (2006). Retrieved on February 12, 2014 from http://www.inst.at/trans/16Nr/01_5/echu16.htm

_____. "The Language Question in Cameroon."(2004). Retrieved January 13, 2012 from http://www.linguistik-online.de/18_04/echu.html

Echu, George and Allan W. Grundstrom. *Official Bilingualism and Linguistic Communication in Cameroon*. New York: Peter Lang, 1999.

Egejuru, Panel A. *Towards African Literary Independence: A Dialogue with Contemporary African Writers*. London: Greenwood Press, 1980.

Ewané, L. M. "Le Camfranglais, Un cousin du Verlan? "*Afrique Elite* 36, (1989): 18-19.

Fanon Frantz. *Black Skin, White Masks*. New York: Grove Press, 1967.

Fanon, Frantz. *Peau noire, masques blancs*. Paris: Editions du Seuil, 1952.

_____. *Les damnés de la terre*. Paris: François Maspero, 1961.

_____. *The Wretched of the Earth*. Trans.Constance Farrington. New York: Grove Press, 1966.

Finnegan, Ruth H. *Oral Literature in Africa*. Oxford: Clarendon, 1970.

_____. *Limba Stories and Story-telling*. Oxford: Clarendon, 1970.

_____. Oral Poetry. Cambridge: Cambridge University Press, 1977.

_____. *The Oral and beyond: Doing Things with Words in Africa*. Chicago: University of Chicago Press, 2007.

Fouda, Mercédès. *Je parle camerounais: pour un renouveau francofaune*.Paris: Karthala, 2001.

Furphy, Joseph. *Such is Life*. London: Angus and Robertson, 1944.

Gandhi, Leela. *Postcolonial Theory: A Critical Introduction*. Edinburg: Edinburg University Press, 1998.

Gates, Henry Louis, Jr. *The Signifying Monkey: A Theory of African-American Literary Criticism*. New York and Oxford: Oxford University Press, 1989.

Genette, Gerard. *Palimpsestes: la littérature au second degré*. Paris: Editions du Seuil, 1982.

_____. *Palimpsests: Literature in the Second Degree*. Trans. Channa Newman and Claude Doubinsky. Lincoln: University of Nebraska Press, 1982.

Gérard, Albert. "Oralité, glottophagie, créolisation: Problématique de la littérature africaine," *Bulletin des séances de l'Academie royale des sciences d'Outre-Mer* 34.2, (1988): 259-269.

Glissant, Edouard. *Le discours antillais*. Paris: Editions du Seuil, 1981.

_____. *Caribbean Discourse: Selected Essays*.Trans. Michael

Gauvin, Lise. *L'écrivain francophone à la croisée des langues*. Paris: Editions Karthala, 1997.

Goody, Jack. *The Domestication of the Savage Mind*. Cambridge: Cambridge University Press, 1987.

_____. *The Interface between the Written and the Oral*. Cambridge: Cambridge University Press, 1987.

Gover, Daniel and John Conteh-Morgan. *The Postcolonial Condition of African Literature*. Trenton: Africa World Press, 2000.

Government of Cameroon. *Constitution of the Republic of Cameroon.* Yaounde: Government Printer, 1996.

Griffiths, Gareth. *A Double Exile: African and West Indian Writing between Two Cultures.*London: Masian Boyers, 1978.

Gyasi, Kwaku, A. "Writing as Translation: African Literature and the Challenges of Translation." Research *in African Literatures* 30.2 (1999): 75-87.

_____. "The African Writer as a Translator: Writing African Languages through French." *Journal of African Studies* 16.2(2003): 143-159.

_____. "Maintaining an African Poetics: Translating in/and African African Literature." *Translation Review* 56 (1998): 10-21.

_____. "Translation as a postcolonial Practice: The African Writer as Translator." Ed. Raoul J. Granqvist.*Writing Back in/and Translation.* Frankfurt: Peter Lang, 2006.

Havelock, Eric A. *Origins of Western Literacy.* Toronto: Ontario Institute for Studies in Education, 1976.

_____.*Literate Revolution in Greece and its cultural Consequences.* Princeton: Princeton University Press, 1982.

House, Juliane. "Of the Limits of Translatability" *Babel* 19.4 (1973): 166-67.

_____. *A Model for Translation Quality Assessment.* Tübingen: Gunter Narr Verlag, 1977.

Irele, Abiola. *The African Experience in Literature and Ideology.* London: Heinemann, 1981.

_____. "The African Imagination." *Research in African Literatures* 21.1 (1990): 49-67.

_____. "Narrative, History, and the African Imagination." *Narrative* 1.2 (1993)

_____. *The African Imagination: Literature in Africa and the Black Diaspora*. Oxford: Oxford University Press, 2001.

Jameson, Frederic. "Third-World Literature in the Era of Multinational Capitalism." *Social Test* 5.3 (1986): 65-88.

Jones, Michelle H. *The Beginning Translator's Workbook or The ABC of French to English Translation*. New York: University of America, 1997.

Julien, Eileen. *Orality through Writing: Les contes d'Amadou Koumba*. Ph.D Dissertation. Madison: University of Wisconsin-Madison, 1978.

_____ *African Novels and the question of Orality*: Bloomington: Indiana University Press, 1992.

Khatibi, Abelkebir. *Amour bilingue*. Montpellier: Fata Morgana, *1983*.

_____*Love in Two Languages*. Trans. Richard Howard. Minneapolis: University of Minnesota Press, 1990.

Kouega, Jean-Paul. Camfranglais: *A Glossary of Common Words, Phrases and Usages*. Muenchem: LINCOM EUROPA, 2013.

_____. "The Slang of Anglophone Cameroonian University Adolescents." *A Glossary. Syllabus* 1(2010a): 88-116.

_____. "Campus English: Lexical Variations in Cameroon." *International Journal of the Sociology of Language,* 199. (2009a): 89-101.

_____. *A Dictionary of Cameroon Pidgin English Usage: Pronunciation, Grammar, and Vocabulary. Muenchem: LINCOM EUROPA,* 2008.

_____.*A Dictionary of Cameroon English Usage.*Berne: Peter Lang, 2007.

_____.*Aspects of Cameroon English Usage: A Lexical Appraisal.* Muenchem: LINCOM EUROPA, 2006.

_____. (2003): "Word formative processes in Camfranglais," *World Englishes* 22-4(2003): 511-539.

_____ (2003): "Camfranglais: A novel slang in Cameroon schools," *English Today* 19-2(2003): 23-29.

_____. "Uses of English in Southern British Cameroons." *World Englishes* 23.1(2002): 93-113.

_____. "Pidgin Facing Death in Cameroon." *Terralingua*. Retrieved on February 15, 2014 from http://www.terralingua.org.

Juneja, Om P. *Postcolonial Novel: Narratives of Colonial Consciousness*. New Delhi: Creative Books, 1995.

Kane, Cheikh H. *L'aventure ambiguë*. Paris: Julliard, 1961.

Kourouma, Ahmadou. *Les soleils des indépendances*. Paris: Editions du Seuil, 1970.

_____.*The Suns of Independence*. Trans. Adrian Adams. NewYork: Africana, Publications, 1981.

_____.Kourouma, Ahmadou. *Monnè : outrages et défis*. Paris : Editions du Seuil, 1990.

_____. *Monnew*. Trans. Nidra Poller. San Francisco: Mercury House, 1993.

_____.*En attendant le vote des bêtes sauvages*. Paris, Édition du Seuil,1998.

Kuitche, F. Gabriel. *Moi taximan*. Paris: L'Harmattan, 2001.

Kunene, Mazisi. "Panel on South African Oral Traditions."*Issue : A Quarterly Journal of Africanist Opinion* 6.1 (1976) : 1-63.

_____. "The Relevance of African Cosmological Systems to African Literature Today." Eds. Eldred Jones et al. *African Literature Today: Myth and History.* London : Heinemann, 1980.

Lawson, A. and Helen Tiffin. *Describing Empire ? Postcolonialism and Textuality.* London: Routledge, 1994.

Lefevere, André. *Translating Literature: Practice and Theory in a Comparative Literature Context.* New York: Modern Language Association of America, 1992.

Lopès, Henri. Le pleurer-rire. Paris: Présence Africaine, 1982.

_____. *The Laughing Cry: An African Cock and Bull Story.* Trans. Gerald Moore. New York : Readers International Inc., 1987.

Lord, Albert. *The Singer of Tales.* New York : Antheneum, 1960.

Mbangwana, P.N. "Invigorative and Hermetic Innovations in English in Yaounde." *World Engishes* 10.1(1991): 53-63.

Mbassi-Manga, Francis. "The State of Contemporary English in Cameroon." Ed. Francis Mbassi-Manga. *Cameroon Studies in English and French* (CASEF).Victoria: Cameroon Press, 1976.

Memmi, Albert. *Portrait du colonisé, précédé du portrait du colonisateur.* Paris: Bucket/Chastel, 1957.

Mendo Zé, Gervais. *Le français langue africaine: Enjeux et atouts pour la Francophonie.* Paris: Publisud, 1999.

Miller, Christopher. *Theories of Africans: Francophone Literature and Anthropology in Africa.* Chicago: The Chicago University Press, 1990.

_____. *Blank Darkness: Africanist Discourse in French.* Chicago: The University of Chicago Press, 1985.

Ndangam, Lillian. "All of us have taken gombo: Media Journalism and Patronage in Cameroonian Journalism." *Journalism* 10.6 (2009): 819-842.

Ndi, Bill. *Toil and Delivery*. Bamenda: Langaa RPCIG, 2010.

_____. *Gods in the Ivory Towers*. Bloomington: AuthorHouse, 2008.

_____. *Waves of Anger*. Maryland: Publish America, 2010.

Ndoutoume, Tsira Ndong. *Le mvett: l'homme, la mort et l'immortalité*. Paris: L'Harmattan, 1993.

Nemser, W. "Systems of Foreign Language Learners." IRAL (*International Review of Applied Linguistics*) 9.2, 1971.

Newmark, Peter. *A Textbook of Translation*. New York: Prentice-Hall, 1988.

Ngugi, wa Thiongo. *Decolonizing the Mind: the Politics of Language in African Literature*. London: J.Currey, 1986.

Nida, E. "A Framework for the Analysis and Evaluation of Theories of Translation," in Brisling, R.W. (ed.) *Translation: Applications and Research,* New York, Gardner, 1976.

Nganang, Patrice. *Temps de chien*. Paris: Serpent à Plumes, 2001.

_____. *Dog Days*. Trans. Amy Baram Reid. Charlottesville: University of Virginia Press, 2001.

Nkosi, Lewis. *Tasks and Masks: Themes and Styles of African Literature*. Essex: Longman, 1981.

Nnolim, Charles E. *Approaches to the African Novel: Essays in Analysis*. London and Lagos: Saros International Publishers, 1992.

Noss, Philip. "The Ideophone in Gbaya Syntax." *Current Approaches to African Linguistics*. Ed. Gerrit J. Dimmendaal. Dordrecht: Foris, 1986.

Ntsobé, André-Marie, George Achu, Edmond Biloa. eds. *Le camfranglais, quelle parlure? Etude linguistique et sociolinguistique*.Francfort: Peter Lang, 2008.

Nyamnjoh, Francis. *Stories from Abakwa*. Bamenda: Langaa Research and Publishing Common Initiative Group, 2007.

──────────────. *The Cameroon GCE Crisis: A Test of Anglophone Solidarity*. Limbe: Nooremac Press, 1996.

Obeng, Gyasi Samuel and Beverely Hartford. *Political Independence with Linguistic Servitude: The Politics about Languages in the Developing World*. New York: Nova Science Publishers, Inc., 2002.

Obiechina, Emmanuel. "Transition from Oral to Literary Tradition." Présence Africaine 63.3 (1967): 140-161.

──────────────. "Problem of Language in African Writing: The Example of the Novel." *The Conch* 5.1-2(1973): 11-28.

──────────────.*Culture, Tradition and Society in the West African Novel*. Cambridge: Cambridge University Press, 1975.

──────────────. *Language and Theme: Essays on African Literature*. Washington D.C.: Howard University Press, 1990.

──────────────. "Narrative Proverbs in the African novel." *Research in African Literatures* 24.4 (1993): 123-140.

Ojo-Ade, Femi. "The Role of the Translator of African Literature in Intercultural Consciousness and Relationships" *Meta* 31.3 (1986): 291-299.

──────────────. "The Literary Translator, Messenger or Murderer? A Study of Oyono's *Une vie de boy* and Reed's *Houseboy*." Ed. Femi Ojo-Ade. *On Black Culture*. Ile-Ife: Obafemi Awolowo University Press, 1989.

Okara, Gabriel. *The Voice*. London: A. Deutsch, 1964.

Okpewho, Isidore. *The Epic in Africa*. New York: Columbia University Press, 1979.

_____. "African Poetry: The Modern Writer and the Oral Tradition." Eds. Jones et al.*Oral and Written poetry in African Literature Today*. Trenton: Africa World Press, 1988.

_____. *The Oral Performance in Africa*. Ibadan: Spectrum Books, 1990.

_____. *African Oral Literature; Backgrounds, Character and Continuity*. Bloomington: Indiana University Press, 1992.

Olaniyan, Tejumola and Ato. Eds. *African Literature: An Anthology of Criticism and Theory*. Oxford: Blackwell Publishing, 2007.

Oluwole, Adejare. "Translation: A Distinctive Feature of African Literature in English."Eds. Epstein, L. Edmund and Robert Kole. *The Language of African Literature*. Trenton: Africa World Press, 1998.

Omole, James O. "Code-switching in Soyinka's *The Interpreters*." Eds. Epstein, L. Edmund and Robert Kole. *The Language of African Literature*. Trenton : Africa World Press, 1998.

Omotoso, Kole. *Combat*. London: Heinemann, 1972.

Ouedraogo, Jean. "An Interview with Ahmadou Kourouma." *Callaloo* 23.4 (2000): 1338-1348.

_____. *Maryse Condé et Ahmadou Kourouma: Griots de l'indicible*. New York: Peter Lang, 2004.

Ouologuem, Yambo. *Le devoir de violence*. Paris: Editions du Seuil, 1968.

_____. *Bound to Violence*. Trans. Ralph Manheim .London: Secker and Warburg, 1971.

Oyono, Ferdinand. *Une vie de boy*. Paris: Julliard, 1956.

———. *Houseboy*. Trans. John Reed. London: Heineman, 1966.

Quayson, Ato. *Post-colonialism: Theory, Practice or Process?* Cambridge: Polity Press, 2000.

Rao, Raja. *Kanthapura*. New York: New Directions, 1938.

Romain, Jacques. *Les gouverneurs de la rosée*.Port-au-Prince. Imprimerie de l'etat, 1944.

Rusdie, Salman. *Imaginary Homelands: Essays and Criticism*. London and New York: Granta Books, 1991.

Said, Edward. *Culture and Imperialism*. London: Chatto and Windus, 1993.

Selinker, Larry. "Interlanguage." In *International Review of Applied Linguistics*10(1972): 209-241.

———. *Rediscovering Interlanguage*. London and New York, Longman, 1992.

Sembène, Ousmane. *Les bouts de bois de Dieu: Banty Mam Yall*. Paris: Le Livre Contempoarain, 1960.

———. *God's Bits of Wood*. Trans. Francis Price. London: Heinemann, 1962.

———. *Vehi-Ciosane ou Blanche–Genèse, suivi du Mandat*. Paris: Présence Africaine, 1965.

———. *Camp de Thiaroye*. New York: New Yorkers Films, 1987.

Shakespeare, William. *The Tempest*. Cambridge: The University Press, 1921.

Simo Bobda, A.*Aspects of Cameroon English Phonology*. Bern: Peter Lang, 1994.

Simo Bobda,A. and Chumbow, B.S. "The Trilateral Process in Cameroon English Phonology." *English World Wide* 20.1 (1999): 35-65.

Slemon, Stephen. "Monuments of Empire: Allegory/Counter-discourse/Postcolonial Writing." *Kunapipi* 9.3(1987b): 1-16.

_____. "Unsettling the Empire: Resistance Theory for the Second World." *English* 30.2(1990): 30-41.

Soyinka, Wole. *The Interpreters*. London: A Deutsch, 1965.

_____. *The Road*. London: Oxford University Press, 1968.

_____. *Ogun Abibidman*. Johannesburg: Raven Press, 1980.

Stokle, Norman. "Toward the Africannization of the African Novel: Francis Bebey's Narrative Technique." Ed. Kolawole Ogungbesan. *New West African Literature*. London: Heinemann, 1979.

Stolz, Benjamin, A. and Shannon Richard (Eds.) *Oral Literature and the Formula*. Ann Arbor: CCMAS, 1976.

Tervonen, Taina. "L'ecrivain a l'ecole de la rue. Entretien avec Patrice Nganang," *Africulture*, No. 37, 2001.

Todd, L. *Modern Englishes: Pidgins and Creoles*. Oxford: Blackwell, 1984.

_____. *Varieties of English around the World TI Cameroon*: Heidelberg: Julius Groos, 1982.

Tremblay, Michel. *Les belles-soeurs*. Montréal: Leméac, 1972.

Tutuola, Amos. *The Palm-Wine Drinkard*. London: Faber and Faber, 1952.

Vakunta, P.W. *Carnet d'un retour au pays natal en camfranglais*. Kindle Edition, 2014.

_____. *Méditations poétiques en camfranglais*. Kindle Edition, 2013.

_____. *A Nation at Risk: A Personal Narrative of the Cameroonian Crisis:* Bloomington: i-Universe, 2012.

_____.*Indigenization in the African Francophone Novel: A New Literary Canon*. New York: Peter Lang Publishers, 2011.

_____. "Ivorian Nouchi, Cousin to Cameroonian Camfranglais" Retrieved on January 16, 2011 from http://www.postnewsline.com/2011/01/ivorian-nouchi-cousin-to-cameroonian-camfranglais.html

_____. "Music, Language and Human Rights in Cameroon: The Voices of Elwood, Valsero and Lapiro." Retrieved November 10, 2011 from http://www.pambazuka.org/en/category/books/77843

_____. *Cam Tok and Other Poems from the Cradle*. Bamenda: Langaa RPCIG, 2010.

_____. "American Gullah, Cousin to West African Pidgin English?" Retrieved June 6, 2010 from http://www.postnewsline.com/2010/06/american-gullah-cousin-to-west-african-pidgin-english.html

_____. *Majunga Tok: Poems in Pidgin English*. Bamenda: Langaa RPCIG, 2008.

_____.*Cry My Beloved Africa: Essays on the Postcolonial Aura in Africa*.Bamenda: Langaa Research and Publishing CIG, 2008.

_____. On Translating Camfranglais and Other Camerounismes." *Meta* 53.4(2008): 942-947.

_____.*African Time and Pidgin Verses*, Pretoria, Duplico, 2001.

Venuti, Lawrence. *Translator's Invincibility: A History of Translation*. NewYork: Routledge, 1995.

Waberi, Abdourahman. *Aux Etats Unis d'Afrique*. Paris: J.C. Lattès, 2006.

_____. *In the United States of Africa.* Lincoln: University of Nebraska Press, 2009.

Walder Dennis. *Postcolonial Literatures in English: History, Language and Theory.* Oxford: Blackwell Publishers Ltd, 1998.

Wendt, Albert. *Lali: A Pacific Anthology.* Auckland: Longman, 1980.

White, Jonathan. *Recasting the World: Writing after Colonialism.* Baltimore: The John Hopkins University Press, 1993.

Zabus, Chantal. "A Calibanic Tempest in Anglophone and Francophone New World Writing." *Canadian Literature* 104 (1985): 35-51.

_____. *The African Palimpsest: Indigenization of Language in the West African Europhone Novel.* Amsterdam: Rodopi, 1991.

Ze, Amvela E. "Reflexions on the Social Implications of Bilingualism in the Republic of Cameroon" In *Epasa Moto* (A Bilingual Journal of Language, Letters and Culture) Buea, Cameroon: The Buea University Center) I (1): 41-61.

Glossary/Glossaire

A
Aboki: friend, soya vendor
Achomo: cake
Achouka or ashuka: deserved punishment
Achouka ngongoli: deserved punishment
Aff: affair/ business/ stuff
Akwara: prostitute
Ala: other
Alamibou: magician/ exorcist/ seer
Allô: lie
Ami-ami: friend
A mor: so mu
Anaconda: posh car
Ancien: name for someone the speaker does not know
Anglo: anglophone in Cameroon.
Anglofou: anglophone
Anuscratie: homosexuality
Aprem: afternoon
Apprenti-sorcier: opposant
Appuyer: have sex
Arki: locally distilled liquor
Arroser: offer drinks to one's friends
Ashawo: prostitute
Assia (ashia): expression of sympathy
Asso: customer
Atangana bread: bobolo
Attaquant: taxi driver assistant
Attaque: front row of seats in a classroom

Attraper quelqu'un le pilon dans le mortier: catch someone red-handed
Au day: today
Awuf: free of charge
Axe lourd: young prostitute

B
Babtou: a white person/European
Back-back: unlawful dealings
Badluck: misfortune
Bagnole: car
Bahat: ill feelings
Bakassi: any dangerous place
Baleine: state official who embezzles public funds
Bami: short for Bamileke
Banga: pot/hemp
Bangala: penis
Banquer: to ditch one's partner
Bao: a rich man
Baptiser: steal by sneaking away with money for a service
Barlok: misfortune
Bateau: market
Baton: sum of one million Francs
Bazo: brand of expensive shoes
Beaucoup beaucoup: in great quantity
Beau-regard: pork or pig
Bebela! gosh!
Bele: unwanted pregnancy
Bendskin: motocyle used for pubic transport
Bendskinneur: driver of a bendskin
Bep-bep: stammerer/ bragging
Beret-kaki: policeman

Beta: better
Better: would rather/ would better
Beurre: girl's lips
Bibliser: ape the speech of white folks
Biblos: white man/European
Bic: male sexual organs
Bifaka: dried herring
Big bro: elder brother
Big katika: high-ranking official/President of the Republic
Big mater: grandmother
Big pater: grandfather
Big reme: grandmother
Big repe: grandfather
Big rese: elder sister
Bindi: young/ younger/junior
Bindiment: slowly/ gently/softly
Bisness: business
Bitakola: bitter kola
Bled: house, country, village
Blem: problem
Bobi: breast/nipple
Bobi-tenap: brassiere
Bobolo: ground cassava
Bok: prostitute
Bolè: finish/end/ run out of
Bolo: job/work
Boma: boa/rich man who flirts with young girls
Bombo: namesake
Bon-blanc: albino
Bonga: dry fish
Boogie: party/night club
Book: gamble with cards

Bordelle: prostitute
Bordellerie: prostitution
Born: to have a baby
Bosco: bouncer
Boss: boss, manger
Bouffer: refuse to pay back money one has borrowed
Bouffeur: glutton
Bro: short for brother
Boule-zero: close-cut hair
Boum: party
Brancher: to dress well
Branché: well-dressed
Break: break, pause, holiday
Brique: sum of one million francs
Bringue: a party
Bro: short brother
Buche: reading
Buga: dry fish
Bugna: car
Bundja: to score
Bumbu: vagina
Buy: to shop, buy
Buyam-sellam: retailer of food crops
Bye: farewell

C

Ca-aa!: interjection expressing surprise
Cacao: young beautiful girl
Cadavéré: dead/ failed project
Cadeau: for free
Café: serious beating
Caillou: something difficult/hard/strenuous

Calculer: to be on the look out for
Calé: pant
Calé-calé: sex between homosexuals
Calékoum: underwear
Callbox: place where a public phone is available, callbox business
Callboxeur: man who does callbox business
Callboxeuse: woman who does callbox business
Calmas: cool down!
Camer: Cameroon
Camerien: Cameroonian
Camp: indoors/ house/room
Canapé écrasiatique: sofa for love-making
Capo: big shot/mogul/ rich man/friend
Capote: condom
Carreau: match, level
Carry le mbele: become pregnant
Cartouche: lecture notes
Cassé: tired/worn out
C'est how? hello! How is it?
Cha: catch someone
Chain: broke
Chaka: shoes
Cham: room
Chambul: room
Champi: champagne
Champicoter: drink champagne
Changement: change
Chango: address term for men whose wives come from the same family
Chantier: public place or restaurant where food and drinks are sold

Chaud: lover/boyfriend
Chaud gars: hot guy/ Paul Biya/ flirt
Chauffer: to have a sexually transmitted disease
Chavoum: gun
Check: think
Chef: chief/uniformed State official/ police/soldier
Chef-ban: gang leader
Chem: shirt
Chercher: to look for
Chercher la nga d'autrui: court a married woman
Chichard: mean person/niggardly person
Chia: chair/post
Chiba: live or reside in a place
Chichard: niggardly or mean person
Chier: to defecate
Choko: bribe/tip
Chomercam: unemployment in Cameroon
Chop: eat
Chopale: sexually transmitted disease
Chop-broke-pot: selfish person
Chop-bluk-pot: selfish person
Chop chia: heir/successor
Chopper: to contract an STD
Christine: economic crisis
Chuker: kick start a car/ have sex
Chuki: trap
Cinema njoh: a free scene
Cinosh: cinema
Circuit: public place or restaurant where food and drinks are sold
Civiliser: lecture someone
Clando: private car illegally used as a taxi

Class: first-class
Clim: air-conditioner
Close: clothes/ make love
Close les eyes: to persevere/ go ahead/igore a difficulty
Coca-alhadji: insult to Muslims who use coke to color alcoholic drinks
Co-chambrier: room-mate
Coco: girlfriend
Coder: prevent people from seeing something
Coller-chewing gum: very tight/ to gum like chewing gum
Coller-coller: dance tune
Coma: cinema
Comb: have sex/make love
Combi: friend
Come-no- go: disease that causes body to itch
Comment? How are you?
Comot: leave/get out/go out
Comot le corrigé de: produce the best example of
Complice: accomplice/friend
Composer: dupe someone
Condol: condolences
Consti: constipated
Copo: friend
Cops: friend
Coraniser: to cram and recite lecture notes
Corrigé: master copy
Corriger: to make love
Cosh: insult/abuse
Cota: friend/male or female partner
Coupé-décalé: type of music from Côte d'Ivoire
Couper: make love
Cou-plié: rich man

Crâner: to show off; to brag
Crayon: penis
Criquer: to threaten somone
Crish: crazy/drunk/berserk
Cut: extort money from people
Cyclis: tights worn as underwear by women

D

Damba: football
Damer: cooked food/to eat food
Damé: cooked food/to eat food
Dangwa: stroll/walk
Day: there is/day
Dash: faire cadeau/ donner
Débat: woman with a broad waist/with big buttocks
Débré: to try/ to somehow manage
Décapsuler: to deflower a girl
Décapsulage: deflowering a girl
De from: since/ever since
Dégager: remove/get rid of
Dégombotiser: fight against corruption
Dem: give up/abandon/ fail/disappoint
Deme: mess/trouble
Démarrage: state of being sexually aroused
Démarrer: to sexually arouse someone
Den: identity card
Depe: homosexual
Déposer: to leave someone alone
Dépose-moi! leave me alone!
Deps: homosexual
Depso: homosexual
Depuis depuis: a very long time ago

Depuis from: since/ever since/ for a very long time
Deuxième bureau: concubine/illegal sex partner
Diabe: diabetic person
Die: suffer/fail
Diva: to ramble/wander/tell stories
Djigi-djaga: noise and cuddling made by people moving love
Djim: big/large
Djim-djim: very big/very large
Djimtété: important person/ mogul/rich person
Djingue: clothes
Djo: friend/partner/man/boy
Djoka: dance/idleness/leisure
Djomba: illegal sex partner/ girlfriend
Djoum: jump
Djuksa: unattractive/horrible
Doc: medical doctor/herbalist
Docta: medical doctor/herbalist
Do: to do/make
Do: money/dough
Do le hon-hon-hon: to brag/show off/tell lies to win favors
Do le java: to the waltz
Do le mapan: to make love
Do le way: make love
Do moh: to enjoy
Do two weeks: to spend two weeks
Doser: to measure out something in the right proportions
Doser quelqu'un: to hit someone repeatedly in a fight
Dossier: girl one intends to chat up
Doucement doucement: very slowly or very gently
Doul: Douala

Dribbler: to play truant
DSK: Dominique Strauss-Kahn
Dur: in a hard way
Dybo: someone/a man/important person

E
Eat: to eat
Eat le do: squander money
Eateur: glutton
Eclater: to enjoy oneself
Ecorce: talisman; fetish
Ecraser: make love with a woman
Ecrasage: love-making
Ecraseur: love-maker
Ecrasiatique: for love-making
Ekié! gosh! Interjection expressing surprise
Elobi: swamp
Engin: male or female sex organ
En haut: to be up or appointed
Erreur: mistake/mishap
Etre: to be
Etre en haut: appointed to a post where one can embezzle State funds
Etre frais: to be in good shape
Etre in: to be sexy/to be fashionable
Etre chaud dans quelqu'un: to be broke
Evou: witchcraft
Evu: witchcraft

F
Fafio: money/fortune
Faire ça dur à quelqu'un: to handle someone roughly

Faire comme ça: farewell expression
Fire le mapan: to make love
Fais quoi, fais quoi: No matter what happens/no matter what you think.
Faire: make love/ have sex
Faire chier: interjection synonymous with gosh!
Faire le hon-hon-hon: to brag/show off/tell lies to win favors
Faire le java: to the waltz
Falla: search for/have the intention of chatting up a girl
Famla: witchcraft/ sorcery/ fetish
Fan: to look for
Fan la nga d'autrui: court someone else's girlfriend
Farotter: give out gifts in cash
Farotteur: saint Nick/ Santa Claus
Faux: false/fake
Faux pass: forged passport
Feel: to feel/have feelings
Fey: feyman/to dupe/fool/deceive/swindle
Feyman: con man
Feymanie: trickery
Fictionner: make love/have sex
Fiesta: party
Fifty-fifty: equal sharing
Fmisé: to hit by economic crisis
Finir: drink too much/be exhausted
Fire: risk/ danger/failure/ fire/trouble/emergency
Flash: dry cough
Flop: many/complete/numerous
Foi: short for foirage
Foirage: state of being broke/poverty/hardship
Foirer: to be broke

Fok: make love
Folon: vegetable dish
Foup-foup: disorder
Fraicheur: young beautiful woman
Frais: in good shape/ financially sound/ elegant
Frangin: village dweller/friend/someone living in the rural area
Frappe: dupery
Frappeur: conman
Fringueur: someone who dresses well
Frog: francophone Cameroonian
Front: reading
Fronter: to read for long
Fuck: copulate/make love

G
Galère: hardship
Galérer: to be facing hard times
Gandura: gown
Garder: to take along a gift
Garer: to stand someone up
Gari: a bribe
Gars: friend/boyfriend
Gata: prison
Gengerou: albino
Gengeru: albino
Gee: give
Gérant: someone who goes out with a girl
Gérer: to go out with a girl
Ghettosard: someone who lives in a poverty-stricken area
Gib: give
Gif: give

Ginger: something difficult to do
Gip: give
Gnama: food/to eat
Gneps: type of cake
Gnole: car
Gombo: bribe/tip
Gombotique: related to corruption
Gombotiser: to give a bribe
Gomna: government/governor/ police officer// manager
Gonfler: to brag/boast
Graf-fo-de: piss off/get lost/to go hell
Grand: elder brother
Grand brother: elder brother
Grand Camarade: El Hajj Ahmadou Ahidjo
Grillé: someone who has nothing to lose
Grimba: witchcraft
Grimbatique: related to witcraft
Grimbatiser: protect property with fetish
Gui: girl
Guitare: type of skin disease

H
Haa: strong home-made liquor
Hala: to hassle/scold/scream
Haba! interjection of surprise
Half-book: illiterate
Haut: up/ high-ranking
Hear: listen/obey
Helele: interjection of surprise
Helep: help
Hia: hear/listen/obey

Hier-hier: novice
Hiish! interjection expressing a feeling of repugnance
Homme-Lion: Lion Man/ Paul Biya/President of Camreroon
Hon-hon-hon: bragging
Hon-hon: to brag
Hosto: hospital
Hot: difficult/busy
Hot la tête: make someone think
How? : Hi
How que? How come?
Hyper: excessive
Hyper hot: very busy

I
ID: identity card
If: if
Il y a match: the stakes are high
Imbook: illiterate
In: in vogue
Intello: intellectual/learned person

J
Jachère: period of loneliness for a girl
Jaka: boyfriend/partner
Jambo: gambling
Jamboteur: gambler
Jamboula: night club
Janga: small/slim/slender/little
Jazz: cooked beans
Jazzer: to eat beans
Jazzeur: someone who eats beans regularly

Jeune talent: young man, young woman
Je wanda: I wonder
Jia: listen/obey
Jobajo: locally brewed beer
Johnny: to pad/tramp/walk
Johnny-Four-Foot: goat/idiot
Joka: a party
Jomba: illegal sex partner/ girlfriend
Jos: judge, discuss, argue
Juju-kalabar: monster/something frightful
Jus: judge, discuss, argue

K
Kaba: gown worn by pregnant women
Kai! Expression of anger
Kamambrou: head of state/leader/chief executive
Kako: girl one is courting
Kamer: Cameroon
Kamerlock: Cameroonian doldrums
K-merlock: Cameroonian doldrums
Kam-no- go: disease that causes one's body to itch
Kanda: testicles/cowhide/ belt
Kan-kan: several/something difficult
Kanda: belt/cowhide
Kapo: mogul/ rich person/ friend
Kassa: term used for northerners in Cameroon
Katakata: cunning/good at deceiving
Katika: boss/director
Keep: to keep
Keep quelqu'un: to take along a gift
Keleng keleng: a local type of spinach
Kenekene: okra/slippery/ a local type of spinach

Kengue: Imbecile/idiot
Kenzo: brand of expensive shoes
Kerenkeren: okra/slippery/ a local type of spinach
Keulan: aim/target
Kick: steal/rob
Kicker: rob/steal
Kickman: thief
Kickwoman: thief
Knack kanda: have sex
Know: master
Koki: meal of beans cake
Kolo: 1000 francs CFA
Kolo-fap: 1500 francs CFA
Komot: come out/ go out
Kondre: nation/country
Kondre talk; vernacular language/mother tongue
Kong: witchcraft
Kongolibon: close-cropped
Kongossa: gossip
Kopo: friend/boyfriend
Kosh: insult
Kota: friend/ female or male partner
K.O: Knock out
Koukouma: high-ranking officer/ President of the Republic
Krenkren: okra/slippery/ a local type of spinach
Krish: mad/crazy
Kumbu: big dish
Kunai-kunia: slowly/gently
Kwat: neighborhood
Kwem: meal of cassava leaves

L

Laf: laugh
Lage: village
Lancer: to head for
Langa: mouth watering
Lass: buttocks
Langua: speak/tell/talk
Lap: laugh
Lep: leave
L'homme Lion: /Lion Man/ Paul Biya
Libérer: agree to make love
Loko: to brag
Lolos: breasts
Lom: to tell lies
Londo: to brag
Long: house/home/residence/room
Long crayon: literate folks/ educated people
Longo-longo: tall and slim
Lookot fire: rubber shoes
Loss: die/misplace
Loss sense: fool
Lookot: watch out
Lourd: financially buoyant
Lys: short for lycee

M

Ma: to think up
Maboya: whore
Mafio: criminal
Mafioso: mafia/dealer/swindler
Magan: witchcraft
Magni: mother of twins

Maguida: Muslim from northern Cameroon
Mainant: now
Malamb: bait
Makalapati: bribe/tip
Makandi: vagina
Make le java: to do the waltz
Mamba: ten thousand francs
Ma mami! Gosh!
Mami-pima: mother's vagina
Mange-mille: corrupt police-officer
Management: items of corruption
Manif: manifestation
Mara: marathon
Manioc: vagina/genitals of a woman
Ma own: mine/my own
Massa: Sir/ Mister/friend
Matango: palm wine
Match: sexual intercourse
Mater: mother
Matin, midi, soir: all the time/ all day
Max: maximum
Maxi: maximum
Maux de poche: shortage of resources/ being broke
Mazembe: bandit
Mbambe: menial job
Mbele: pregnancy
Mbeng: Europe
Mbengue: Europe
Mbengueter: travel regularly abroad
Mbeuh! What a pity!
Mbindi: small/junior/young
Mbit: penis

Mboa: country/Douala
Mbom: man
Mbombo: homonym/namesake
Mbourou: money
Mbout: idiot/fool
Mboutoucou: idiot/fool
Mboutman: idiot/fool
Meder: Mercedez car
Megan: witchcraft/fetish
Mémé: young beautiful girl
Même-même: precisely
Même père, même mère: nuclear siblings
Meng: die/kill
Merco: Mercedes car
Merco, gombo, dodo: hustle and bustle of city life.
Metosh: half- breed/light-skinned person
Mettre quelqu'un en haut: appoint someone to a high position
Meuf: young girl one desires
Milito: soldier
Mimbo: liquor
Mimboland: Cameroon
Mingri: slender/slim/skinny
Minion: appetite
Mini minor: woman of small build
Mof-me-de: piss off
Moh: very good/satisfactory
Mola: man/fellow
Molo: gently
Molo-molo: very gently/slowly
Mome: young girl/woman in general
Money-man: rich person

Mon type: man/ someone whose name is forgotten
Mop: mouth
Mortier: female sexual organ/vagina
Motivation: bribe/tip
Mougou: fool/idiot
Mouiller: sexually arouse
Moumie: young beautiful girl one desires
Moyen: financial resources
Mua: add/raise
Mukala: albino/mulatto
Mukwaye: witchcraft/fetish
Mulongo: whip
Mumu: deaf and dumb/stupid person/coward
Mutmut: gnat
Muna: kid/girlfriend

N

Na: it is
Na how? hello! how is it?
Nack: to tell
Nack les divers: chat/gossip
Nak: beat
Nalie!: It's not true!
Nang: sleep/spend the night
Nanga-boko: dirty, filty person
Nassara: white person
Nayor: slowly
Nayor-nayor: very slowly/very gently
Nchinda: page/servant
Ndamba: football match
Ndeme: mess/trouble
Ndiba: water

Ndolo: love
Ndole: national vegetable dish
Ndoleiser: to eat a dish of ndole
Ndombolo: fat/stout woman/fat buttocks
Ndomo: fight
Ndopa: cigarette/tobacco
Ndos: smart person
Ndoutou: ill-luck/bad luck
Ndutu: ill-luck/bad luck
Negos: negotiation
Ness: business
Nga: girl/female partner
Ngata: prison
Ngataman: prisoner
Ngi: female partner/girl
Ngo: girl
Ngo: short for Ongola
Ngola: Cameroon
Ngomna: government
Ngondele: young girl
Ngueme: poverty
Ngum: strength/power
Ngui: female partner/girl
Niama niama: small/ of little value/worthless/useless person
Nian: sell one's personal belongings
Nian-nian: brand new
Niang! : expression of defiance
Nianga: stylish/well-dressed
Nie: see
Nindja: police man/soldier
Nioxer: have sex/fuck

Njoh: free of charge
Njoka: a party
Njoter: free of charge
Njoteur: opportunist
Nkane: prostitute
Nkap: money/fortune/resources
Nkui: meal of brownish color
Noyaux: testicles
Now now so: right now/right away
Ntamulung choir: useless noise/brouhaha
Ntong: luck/opportunity
Nucer: suck a girl's lips/kiss a girl passionately
Nyama nyama: very small/ of little significance or value
Nye: see
Numéro six: intelligence/perspicacity

O

Obosoh! gosh!
O'day: today
Odontol: locally distilled liquor
Okrika: second-hand clothes
On fait comme ça: Ok, see you later!
Oncal: uncle
One man show: bragging/boasting
Ongola: Cameroon/Yaounde
Ongolais: Cameroonian
On vous connaît! We know how dishonest you are!
Opep: private car used illegally for transporting passengers
Opposant: member of an opposition party
Ordi: computer
Organe de base: male genital organs

Over: too much
Oya: oil/grease

P
Pacho: father
Pa Pol: Paul Biya
Padre: Prêtre
Paff: corn pap
Palava: affaire
Pample-porc: grapefruit and pork
Paplé: surprised/unbelievable/unthinkable/mad
Parler: give a bribe/corrupt a public official
Pass: passport
Pater: father
Pays-bas: genital organs
Pederastie: gay practices
Penia: new
Penya penya: very new/ in very good state
Pep: leave/go away
Pepe: girlfriend
Pepper: hot/difficult
Perfusion: drip
Perika: Petit frère
Petite: girlfriend
Piak: to sneak away
Piaule: residence/apartment
Pif: fall in love
Pilon: male sexual organ/penis
Piol: residence/apartment
Piole: residence/apartment
Pipo: people
Pistachage: love-making

Pistache: female genital organ/vagina
Pistacheur: love-maker
Pistachique: related to love-making
Plantain: male genital organ/penis
Pointage: paid menial job
Pointer: do a paid menial job
Politiquart: politician
Popol: Paul Biya/President of Cameroon
Pote: mate/friend
Potopoto: mud/low-cost house built with mud
Pousseur: truck pusher
Poum: sneak away
Pratiquer: practice occult rituals
Prendre quelqu'un le pilon dans le mortier: catch someone red-handed
Preso: condom
Pression: pressure
Pro: problem/professional
Probat: secondary school certificate

Q
Quat: neighborhood/ quarter/residential area
Quata: neighborhood/ quarter/ residential area
Quartier: neighborhood/ quarter/ residential area
Quota: male or female partner/friend

R
Radio trottoir: rumor
Rangers: type of strong canvas shoes
Raser: disgrace someone
Rationner: provide money for food
Reach: arrive/reach

Reback: return/ come back/go back/resume
Recame: return/ come back/go back/resume
Rdépéciste: member of the CPDM in Cameroon/member of the ruling party
Refre: brother
Rego: return/ come back/go back
Reme: mother
Renault-deux: walk/tramp/trek
Repe: father
Rese: sister
Ricain/recaine: American
Rond: money
Rythmer: go out with a girl but not make love with her
Rythmeur: someone who goes out with a girl but does not make love with her

S
Sabitout: know-all
Sabi: know
Saccager; make love exhaustively
Saka: dance/go to a nightclub
Salaka: sacrifice
Samara: sandals made of cow hide
Sango: man/sir
Sansanboy: smart boy/young lad
Sans-con: rubber-made slippers
Sans-payer: a police-van
Sapak: whore
Sapeur: someone who dresses well
Saper: dress well
Sara: white man/woman
Saraka: sacrifice

Sauveteur: street hawker
Science: think/ponder
Secteur: spot where hawkers sell their goods
Sentir quelqu'un: feel someone's ruthlessness/power
Se sucrer: to embezzle public funds
Seven plus one: AIDS
Sexy: see through outfit
Shaba: war-torn/poverty-stricken
Shake: to dance
Shap: early morning
Shap shap: very early in the morning
Sherif: rich man
Shiba: live/reside in a place
Show le pepper: to trouble/disturb
Siba: live/reside in a place
Silencieux: 100 CFA francs
Sissia: intimidate someone
Sista: sister
Sita: sister
Sitak: taxi
Situass: occasion/event
Small: minor
Small no be sick: popular Chinese balm
Sortir le corrigé de: produce the best example of
Sotuc: prostitute
Soya: roasted meat sold near pubs
Sous-quat: ghetto/slum
Souteneur: boyfriend or husband
States: USA
Stationnement: parking
Statois: someone who has been to the USA
Story: gossip

String: type of female dress
Sucre: girlfriend
Swa: fear
Swit-mimbo: pop/soda
Swine: abuse term
Swolo: swallow
Squatter: to live/stay

T
Taco: taxi
Tanap: stand up
Tara: complice
Taff: cigarette
Tagne: father of twins
Tailler: run away
Tai-toi: bribe
Takesh: taxi
Tango: soft beverage obtained by adding some syrup to beer
Tanner: make love exhaustively
Tantal: aunt/any sister or half-sister
Tantine: aunt
Tara: friend
Tarcler: foul play in soccer
Taxi-opep: private car used illegally for transporting passengers
Tcha: catch someone red-handed
Tcha quelqu'un le pilon dans le mortier: catch someone red-handed
Tchango: address term for men whose wives come from the same family
Tchat: chat up a girl

Tchatcher: chat up a girl
Tchatcheur: some who knows how to enterain women
Tchoko: tip/bribe
Tchotchoro: small/not mature
Tchouquer: jump start a car/make love
Tchouqueur: womanizer
Tchouki: domain under one's control
Teboi: nightclub
Tell: recount/ tell/alert/inform
Tempo: watch out!
Tensionner: anger/bother
Terma: mother
Terminer: make love exhaustively
Terpa: father
Testo: testicles
Tété: important person/rich man
Tif: thief/steal
Timor: bully
Timoriser: to bully/frighten
Titi: girl
Titulaire: preferred girlfriend
Titus: preferred girlfriend
Tobassi: charm/spell/mystical power
Tok: talk/speak
Tokio: run away
Toli: gossip/story
Tong: luck/opportunism
Tonner: to abuse/insult
Tonton: uncle/respectable person
Top: first class
Topo: story/talk
Tori: gossip/story

Tosh: begging for a stick of cigarette
Tosher: beg for a stick of cigarette
Toshme: half-breed
Toum: sell one's personal belonging
Tourne-dos: turn-back restaurant/ makeshift restaurant
Tracer: go away
Trois V (travail, villa, virement): car, house, bank transfer.
Troisième pied: penis
Truanteur: thief
Tuber: tuberculosis
Tuyau: bribe channel/nightclub
Tuyauriste: party-goer
Type: man whose name the speaker doesn't know

U
Understand: to understand
Up: short for up-eye/bullying

V
Vass: to wash
Vendre: to sell
Vendre quelqu'un au famla: bewitch someone
Vendre quelqu'un au kong: bewitch someone
Vendre quelqu'un au nyiongo: bewitch someone
Ventre: witcraft/stomach
Verber: talk/chat
Vere: dream
Vernis haoussa: Hausa vanish
Vesté: wearing a suit
Viens-on-reste: living together but not married
Vieux: father/parents
Villakonkon: uncivilized person/rustic

Villaps: uncivilized persons/rustics
Voisin: neighbor whose name one does not know
Voiso: neighbor
Voum: bragging
Vrai-de-dieu! : By God!
Vrai-vrai: truly

W

Wanda: wonder/be surprised
Wadjax: Muslim from one of the three northern regions of Cameroon
Wadjo: Muslim from one of the three northern regions of Cameroon
Wah: woman or girl one desires
Wai: address term for someone from the northern part of Cameroon
Waka: walk/stroll/function/girl searching for a husband
Walai! interjection expressing anger
Wangala (variant of bangala): male genital organ
Wash: take a bath
Way: means/money
White: European
Win: succeed
Wok: work/job
Wolowoss: prostitute
Wowo: bad/not attractive

Y

Ya: hear/listen
Ya: your
Ya moh: enjoy/be satisfied
Ya bad: suffer

Yam: yam
Yam-fufu: pounded fresh yam eaten with soup
Yelo pepe: type of pepper
Yemale! : Gosh!
Youa: your
Yua: your
Yus: use
Yusles: useless
Yuropian: whiteman/European
Yut: youth
Yi: his/her/its
Yi on: his/her/its own
Yo: young boy that dresses up well
Yoh: young boy that dresses up well
Yoyette: young girl that dresses up well

Z
Zamba: God
Zamzam: very big/very large
Zangalewa: soldier
Zapper: ditch a lover
Zhon: drunk
Zik: short for music
Zikmu: short for music
Ziro: zero
Zoroh: allowing the ball to pass between one's legs in a game of soccer
Zouazoua: fuel of doubtful origin/ illicit fuel sold clandestinely in Cameroon

Index

A

Abrogation 13
Acculturation 42
Achebe 30, 31, 32, 39, 40, 43, 45, 163
Achu 12
Africa 14, 16, 32
Africanism 21, 112
African literaturen=African literature137, 140
Africanization 148
Alterity 3, 24
Aphorism 43
Appropriation 13, 18, 24, 28, 52, 109
Ashcroft 2, 3, 7, 18, 23

B

Badday 88
Bamileke 68, 77, 143
Bamoun 138
Bamunka 138
Bantu 68
Bardolph 1, 2
Bebey 146, 147, 148, 149, 161, 162
Belinga 142
Bhaba 9, 44, 145
Bilingualism 41, 59
Biloa 12, 71, 72
Bislama 94
Bobolo 127

Boni 18, 19
Bororo Kamtok 119
Burlesque 117
Bwa language 18, 19
Bwamu 18

C

Caliban 5, 7, 8
Cameroon 9, 12, 13, 30, 31
Cameroonian literature 133, 135, 150
Camfranglais 12, 33, 41, 57, 59, 60, 61, 63, 64, 66, 72, 73
Camfranglophone 41, 60, 64, 67, 74, 77
Camspeak 59
Canon 24
Césaire 7
Chamoiseau 35, 36, 37, 38, 39
Chamoisification 36
Chevrier 146
Choko 70
Code-mixing 107
Code-switching 27, 57, 61, 86 111, 114, 117
Colonialism 1, 2, 31, 49
Colonization 1, 2, 3
Confiant 163
Congo 19
Creole 30, 36, 37, 39
Cross-cultural criticism 3
Cross-cultural textuality 23
Culture 1
Cultural dualism 47
Cultural identity 65
Cultural imperialism 6, 81

Cultural relativism 27

D
Decolonization 13, 40, 52, 56, 57
Discours antillais 36
Dissent 5
Domestication 19, 85, 131
Duala 125, 126, 130, 147

E
Echu 71, 72
Egejuru 91
Empire 48, 50
Ethnographic novel 102
Ethnographic text 42
Ethnolect 82
Ethno-text 42, 149
Estrangement 47

F
Famla 68, 77, 124
Fanti 29
Finnegan 136, 144
Folklore 27
Fonkou 26, 43, 95, 97, 103, 151
Foreign language 4
Fouda 11, 12, 81, 84, 85, 93
Francophone 6, 7
Francophonie 164
Francophone identity 36
Francophone literature 6, 7, 55
French 36

Fulbe 69
Fulfulde 68, 69, 122
Fulani 68
Furphy 27

G
Gandhi 9
Gates 79, 125
Gauvin 157, 158, 163
Gendarme 12
Gérard 10, 106
Glissant 163
Globalization 34
Glottophagia 162
Gombo 83
Gover 11
Grafi kamtok 119
Griffiths 3, 9, 11
Griot 134,149
Griotization 149
Gullah 29
Gyasi 108

H
Hybrid code 28, 34
Hybrid language 9, 34
Hybrid literature 2
Hybridity 28, 50
Hybridization 50
Hybridized language 160

I
Ideophone 66
Idiom 140
Igbo 29, 31, 43, 46
Imperial language 13, 24, 29
Imperial power 3
Imperialism 5, 39, 56
Indigenization 16, 17, 26, 38, 47, 50, 85, 129, 140
Indigenous language 128, 129, 159
Innovation 26
Inscription 24
Interlanguage 71
Interpolation 86
Interpretation 86
Intra-lingual translation 54, 85
Irele 21, 144

J
Jameson 11
Jazz 74, 116

K
Kabba 102
Kamtok 119
Koki 126
Kouega 10, 34, 35, 59, 62, 66, 76, 97, 100, 103
Kourouma 16, 88, 101, 111
Krio 162

L

Language 8
Language mixing 34
Lawson 11
Limbe kamtok 119
Linguistic imperialism 6
Linguistic hybridity 75
Linguistic indigenization 17
Linguistic plurality 45, 122
Linguistic variance 50
Lingala 20
Lopès 19, 21, 20

M

Malinke 16, 17
Mbangwana 59
Medùmba 14, 112, 124, 125
Memmi 9
Mendo Ze 98
Metonymy 23, 51, 64
Miller 137
Mphahlele 90
Mongo Beti 139
Mvett 139
Multiculturalism 32

N

Narrative technique 43
Nationalism 19
Nemser 26
Neologism 12, 86, 97, 98
Nganang 14, 31, 32, 82, 109, 111, 125

Ngugi 4
Nkosi 140
Ntsobé 12, 71, 72, 74, 76, 78
Nyamnjoh 32, 33, 34

O

Obiechina 154
Ojo-Ade 88
Okara 14
Okpewho 142
Olaniyan 5
Ong 142
Orality 133, 135, 136, 151
Oral literature 136, 142, 155
Oral tradition 27 142, 152
Otherness 23
Oyono 54

P

Palimpsest 106
Papua New Guinea 29
Parallelism 66
Phonology60
Pidgin 29, 30, 31, 92
Pidgin English 64, 72, 77, 103, 104, 105
Pidginized English 26
Pidgin French 59
Pidginization 120, 123
Plurality 30
Plurilingualism115
Polysemy 62
Postcolony 1

Postcolonialism 1, 2, 45
Postcoloniality 1, 2, 47
Postcolonial literature 8, 9, 18, 23, 40, 44, 50
Postcolonial theory 24
Postcolonial writing 27
Prospero 5, 6
Proverb 43, 53, 134, 153

Q
Quayson 5, 9, 45

R
Rao 24, 25
Reduplication 30, 86, 121
Romain 163
Rusdie 9

S
Said 9, 48
Scheub 100, 133
Selinker 26
Semantics 62
Semantic shift 60, 73
Sembene 54
Shakespeare 5, 6
Simile 51
Sociolect 82,122
Sociological novel 101
Soya 10
Soyinka 4
Streetwise French 111, 130
Stylistics 32

Syncretism 47
Synecdoche 51

T
Tervonen 114
Textuality 24
Tiffin 3, 18, 50
Tok Pisin 29
Tremblay 82
Translation 24, 26, 40, 43, 51, 53, 57, 131
Transposition 116
Tutuola 26, 27, 55

U
Untranslatability 131

V
Vakunta 29
Variance 18, 28, 50
Venuti 81
Verlan 67
Vernacular 30, 99

W
Waberi 48, 49
Walder 29
White 11
Witchcraft 124

Y
Yoruba 14, 27, 43, 55
Yoruba imagination 43

Z
Zabus 162
Zamba 15
Ze Amvela 114
Zulu 154

www.ingramcontent.com/pod-product-compliance
Lightning Source LLC
Chambersburg PA
CBHW021943290426
44108CB00012B/947